GSD

08

Platform

An Archeology of the Present

Mohsen Mostafavi
Dean
Alexander and Victoria Wiley Professor of Design

Utopias afford consolation: although they have no real locality there is nevertheless a fantastic, untroubled region in which they are able to unfold; they open up cities with vast avenues, superbly planted gardens, countries where life is easy, even though the road to them is chimerical. –Michel Foucault, *The Order of Things*

A school of the size and characteristics of the GSD is de facto also the location of many projects, research endeavors, events, *utopias*. How then to present any consistencies–logics–amid this array of activity and production?

This publication is an attempt to do just that–to seek the formation of a number of prevalent tendencies, and coherences, among the many that currently operate within the school. Therefore it represents a specific set of choices, a point of view. It takes a stance. But in configuring its inclusiveness it has also had to leave out things, to edit. All for the sake of constructing the clarity of an archeology, one that according to Foucault's schema manifests a history of its conditions of possibility.

The book's content groupings are the site of relations between a diverse range of projects. Even though each of these projects has occurred in different spatial and temporal situations, each grouping produces a new set of experiences out of the propinquity of the chosen subjects and areas of investigation. Seeking such underlying affinities is an important part of the articulation of the school's domains of research. A relational condition develops out of the reading between the various types of projects, events, and writings. The amalgam of all these issues is a partial section of ideas and interests–an archeology of the present state of the school.

This book is not a mere recording of the achievements of our students and faculty, of our lectures, publications, and exhibitions, but an unraveling of an order. It is the site of new, intrinsic experiences and discoveries.

Introduction
Lluis Ortega

This volume presents the research activity of the Harvard Graduate School of Design developed during the 2007–2008 academic year. An inclusive collection of studio work, research seminars, lectures, and other cultural activities, the curation of research "folders" across architecture, landscape architecture, and urban design and planning allows us to identify the most relevant topics of today's and tomorrow's disciplines. GSD 08 Platform constitutes a body of work that is—like design itself—highly complex and dynamic.

The book is organized around a double structure that is reflected in the graphic organization of the book. The first structure is based on "folders," presented on a white background, where contents have been displayed according to their capacity to build a body of knowledge around a particular topic or question. At a moment when it is difficult if not impossible to find totalizing narratives that can direct architectural discussion, but rather a multiplicity of voices and interests, the criteria of this organization has not been established a priori or with a prescriptive attitude, but instead attempts to post-rationalize the diverse work of the school. Individual folders put emphasis on Techniques, on Nature, on the Non-Formal, on Typology, on Geographies, on Technology, on Material, or on reflections on the Discipline. Of course, none of the works included have been established purely in these terms; clustering them under these common umbrellas, however, allows us to reformulate transversal questions about the status and the future of the profession. The constitution of these topics reflects an ambition to understand the discipline as a cultural activity, where innovation is propelled by revisiting old questions and by inventing new terms. This process requires an open mind that embraces the full complexity of the discipline with a lack of prejudices about its internal constitution and techniques.

The second structure of the book is more graphic, based on a series of "booklets" located between the different themes. Each of the booklets between the folders has a distinct color; this differentiation improves the legibility of the organization of the book and reflects the plurality of voices it contains. These pages separate and link the research content of the folders, hosting other materials that gravitate around it: sometimes constituting its foundation, sometimes affected by it, sometimes influencing it, or sometimes simply as commentary. These interferences have a double goal: to avoid reading the body of research content as a linear monochord, and at the same time aggregating the discrete results of the increasing specialization of the profession. Their role, therefore, is to produce a continuous differentiation within what otherwise would be simply a discrete collection. Without any ambition to present a comprehensive narrative or a totalizing legibility, the very fact of having a foundation—a specific disciplinary body of knowledge to transmit, preserve, and expand—is what allows the more speculative work of the research to take place.

GSD 08 Platform

3
An Archeology of the Present
Mohsen Mostafavi

5
Introduction
Lluis Ortega

8
Techniques

Excerpt:
New Things
George Legendre

12
Experiments in Tessellation: The Airport Terminal
Farshid Moussavi

18
Super Tall: Performance and Atmosphere
Hani Rashid

24
The Grid as an Organizational Device for the Design of the City
Joan Busquets, Felipe Correa

30
Excerpt: SUPER
Sarah Whiting

32
Core I Architecture, Fall 2007
Project 1: Lodge House

34
Core I Architecture, Fall 2007
Project 2: Double Door

36
Core I Architecture, Fall 2007
Project 3: Triple Dormer

38
Thesis, Spring 2008
Smooth City: Reinhabiting Chicago's West Loop
Daniel Spiegel

39
Thesis, Spring 2008
GreyMatters: Differential Surface Interactions
Joshua Dannenberg

40
Nature

Excerpt:
What Is Life?
Sanford Kwinter

44
Ecology. Synergy. Design
Behnisch Architekten, Transsolar Climate Engineering

46
28 Questions
Erwan Bouroullec, Rowan Bouroullec

50
Natural and Urban, Green and Grey?
Studies on Specifications of Contemporary Urban Architecture
Inès Lamunière

56
Excerpt:
The Nature of Green in the Yellow Landscapes of Bahrain
Gareth Doherty

60
Core II Architecture, Spring 2008
Project 1: Fenway Station/ ICA

62
Core II Architecture, Spring 2008
Project 2: Allston Research Institute

66
Thesis, Spring 2008
Avoiding Atlantis: Reconstituting Place in an Age of Global Warming
Sun-Young Park

67
Thesis, Spring 2008
The Zorrozaurre Zoological Garden of Cladistics: Heterogeneous Surface Continuity Through Digital Sculpting
Chris Shusta

68
Non-Formal

Excerpt: Levittown
Retrofitted: An Urbanism Beyond the Property Line
Teddy Cruz

74
Dirty Work: Transforming Landscape in the Non-Formal City of the Americas
Christian Werthmann, John Beardsley

80
Reclaiming Utopia: Reality and Initiative in the City of Nairobi
Chi-Yan Chan, Emily Farnham, Sondra Fein, Benny Ho, Meehae Kwon, Yusun Kwon; Jacques Herzog, Pierre de Meuron, advisors

86
Excerpt: NOW?
Abdou Maliq Simone

92
Core III Architecture, Fall 2008
Boston Greenway YMCA

98
Thesis, Spring 2008
Our New Capitol
Bryan Boyer

99
Thesis, Spring 2008
Metrocosm: City in the Sprawl | Stage One: The Catalytic Metamorphosis of the Shopping Mall
Duy Ho

100
Typology

Verticalism (The Future of the Skyscraper)
Iñaki Abalos

104
Urban Sports Culture: A New Stadium for Club Atlético Boca Juniors
Jorge Silvetti

110
Slanted Memorial: Housing For Separated Families at the DMZ, Korea
Jin Young Song

116
Core IV Architecture Spring 2008
Housing

122
Thesis, Spring 2008
[Re] Activating the Senses Within a Blurred Contemporary Reality: Site Specific Apertures
Justin Szeremeta

123
Thesis, Fall 2008
Production and Performance: An Approach to Discarded Landsites on Industrial Waterfronts
Jonathan Rule

4

eographies

esign, Agency,
rritory—Provisional
otes on Planning
d the Emergence of
andscape
arles Waldheim

8

ew Geographies:
esign, Agency, Territory
yran Turan, editor-in-chief

0

ue Architecture of
eography: Istanbul,
ixed-Use Development,
d the Panoramic
ondition
shim Sarkis

6

ue Tenth Aga Khan
ward Cycle
mi Bhabha

2

eservation: Operations
d Mechanisms
fne Bozkurt, Landon Brown,
rren Chang, Dina Ge, Chris
lato, Lisa Su, Lindsay Wai;
m Koolhaas, advisor

8

tudio, Spring 2008
bon: European Atlantic Capital
dolfo Machado

9

tudio, Spring 2008
e Urban Roles of a Semi-Dry
ver: Chihuahua &
Chuvuscar River
ex Krieger

0

ore II Urban
anning,
oring 2008
oject 1: Red Hook
oject 2: Concord

2

ore Elements of Urban
esign, Fall 2007
oject 1: Methuen

3

ore Elements of Urban
esign, Fall 2007
oject 2: Newton

4

ore Elements of
rban Design, Fall 2007
oject 3: Fenway

156

Technology

Critical Digital:
What Matter(s)?
Kostas Terzidis

162

Construction
Automation
Martin Bechthold

164

Surfacing Stone:
Digital Explorations
in Masonry Curtain
Wall Design
Martin Bechthold,
Wes McGee,
Monica Ponce de Leon

172

Responsive Skin
Michael Harris,
David Jaubert;
Toshiko Mori, advisor

174

Stack City
Behrang Behin

180

Core I Landscape
Architecture,
Fall 2007
Somerville High School

181

Core II Landscape
Architecture,
Spring 2008
Brandeis University

182

Core III Landscape
Architecture,
Fall 2007
West Concord

184

Core IV Landscape
Architecture,
Spring 2008
Field's Point, Providence

186

Studio, Spring 2008
Asphalt: The Good,
The Bad, and The Ugly
Paula Meijerink

187

GSD Green Roof
Initiative

188

Material

Excerpt: Systems
For Inclusion
Shigeru Ban

196

Soft Space:
Agile Involution
Sustainable Strategies
for Textile Architecture
Sheila Kennedy

202

Materials
Constructions
Processes
Building in Wood,
Building in Steel
Jonathan Levi,
Thomas Schroepfer

212

Thesis, Spring 2008
Reinterpreting
Governor's Island
Ann Ha

213

Thesis, Spring 2008
Inverting Normals:
A Waterfront Park for
Seoul Ki Duck Kim

214

Lectures 2007–08

215

Student Group
Lectures
2007–2008

216

GSD Publications
2007–08

218

GSD Materials
Collection

220

Discipline

Excerpt: Jacques
Herzog and Peter
Eisenman
Jeff Kipnis, moderator

226

Paradise Extension:
True Confessions
of a 21st-Century
Objectivist
Mack Scogin

230

Excerpt:
The Pipeline:
Power,
Infrastructure,
Territory
Rania Ghosn

234

Excerpt:
The Evolution of
Designers as
Global Actors in
Fast-Growing Cities
of the "Rest"
Shelagh McCartney

238

Excerpt: NOW?
Arjun Appadurai

242

Faculty /
Staff List

250

Credits

Techniques

Excerpt: New Things

George Legendre
Lecture, October 30, 2007

I taught at the Harvard GSD from the mid-1990s until 2000; since then I have been living in London as a practicing architect, formerly a full-time academic. At the school where I teach now, studio faculty like me are given a great deal of freedom to teach essentially whatever we want, to a degree probably unheard of anywhere else—yet, for some reason, all of us end up doing more or less exactly the same thing. And whatever that thing is, it basically has something to do with a surface.

Across this regime of uniformity, however, there are in fact notable differences. As an example, allow me to replay briefly the process of making a material surface as seen from the perspective of two imaginary individuals coming from two very different groups.

In one method the initial idea generally takes the form of a material model made of plasticene, where the maker places it on a workbench, and using a steel ruler and a penknife, he carves straight lines onto its surface. The process is then repeated in the other direction. So each discrete cell is labeled in a proto-indexical manner, in a sort of game board, and every part of the model inscribed in this manner. The maker places, then, the scarred model on a cutting mat, and takes a good whack at it with a seesaw, slicing it in neatly cut parts. Using soft foam and nails, he assembles an elementary pushpin device, and uses it to measure the distance between gridlines and the underside of that handmade machine. He also notes down the length of each pin, and labels it by index. Later, he returns to those measurements to draw the profile of each plasticene on the mat board. He then cuts the profile out, and places it on a mat to double-check on the measurements. He stacks the profiles up, and ponders the pile. Finally, keeping an eye on what's coming up next, he notches each profile to facilitate the assembly. The plasticene surface is put back together again, and the process repeated along the other direction. The newly-made profiles slide gently through one another, and the surface finally appears.

The second method—my method—begins completely differently. There is no seminal idea to work from—only intuitions, and a working knowledge of spatial transformations. These are more like abstract relations between sort of given forms, and they are often expressed with mathematical symbols. They can produce effects of uniformity, non-uniformity, singularity, or any combination thereof. The maker chooses a transformation—say, linearity—pores over her mathematical worksheets, and cobbles together some equations to write a three-dimensional surface plot. Once the equations are written, she can modulate the form of the surface in any dimension and adjust the ranges to thicken the texture. Later, she grinds the surface into point coordinates and exports it into graphical software that turns the numbers into lines, a little bit like beads on a string. The lines are there turned into solid geometry, and if a high-end printing system is available, they are sent to a numerically controlled station that checks them for validity. The process is repeated several times, and may last well into the night. At some point, however, the system will accept the valid RTL model, and fit it to a 3D printing device.

I am sure you all know the machine which basically rolls out coats of plaster, gradually laminating the form by dispensing binding matter over the surface of the plaster. With every new iteration a fresh coat is applied, the layer is bound, and the emergent form sinks a bit deeper into the tank. When the process is complete, the powder is collected for recycling, and the surface form will finally appear. Now, in practice, it doesn't actually happen like this. You actually have to exhume it carefully out of the tank, usually with the help of a specialized technician. When it's finally unearthed, the surface is brushed and cleaned, sometimes mechanically, because it's strengthened with superglue. And as you all know, the tolerance of the machine is absolutely astonishing.

The two methods are obviously different. But what are those differences really about? Or to put it directly, are these differences truly significant? How do the two form-giving strategies really compare? There are a number of ways of going about the comparison, from the crudest to the most refined. You could say, for instance, that the first method is about making big surfaces, whereas the limitations of the machinery force me to make rather small ones. You could put out that one method doesn't actually use the computer—whereas my students and I cannot do anything at all without turning on the machine. I am being a bit facetious, of course, because in actuality, the computer is central to both agendas, though strictly in keeping with both respective sensibilities towards matter. You see, when in the first method one delves under the hood of the system, it's typically to tamper with the physical integrity of the motherboard. The matter lover is typically a hardware man. When I delve under the hood, it is to solve some functional algorithmic intricacy. The matter hater is more likely to be a software guy. The so-called new technologies have their material/immaterial divide, too.

Continuing with this comparison, you cannot help but notice that in the first method the maker chooses to begin with materials, whereas I choose to begin with symbols and scratches on paper. Because the first thinks about materiality effectively through matter and materials, you may deduce that he is some kind of material empiricist, in contrast to the rationalistic, perhaps even the metaphysical, nature òf my approach. By "metaphysical," I mean it literally—"beyond experience." You will also notice that the protagonist of the first method seems to know a lot about casting, woodworking, and the tools of the woodworker, and that he knows how to work with his hands; compared to which my meta-mechanical equipment, with its sanitized and somewhat surgical look, may strike you as vaguely prosthetic. The first, it seems, is of a robust and crafty make, and I of a rather anemic and effete sort. Or, it could actually be exactly the other way around. Depending on whether you value material craft or not, you may, somewhere in the back of your mind, entertain the thought that the first is rather primitive, and I rather developed.

These comparisons may be flawed or correct to some degree or other, but the essential difference between the two approaches is a lot simpler. While the first operates after the surface, as it were, I operate before it. One creates something out of something, if you like, whereas I create something out of nothing. How is that?
Well, the survey of the plasticene does not only have a transferential significance; I borrow these long words from Erwin Panofsky, who uses it to describe the work of the copyist. It is not simply transferring dimensions from one canvas to another; it is also looking for the kind of measurements that will bring a brand new artifact into being. In Panofsky's terms again, this use of measurements is largely constructional, and thus the plasticene original of the example is just a contrivance of this chosen technique, just like the chisel, the pushpin, or any other utensil involved in the process.

I see things completely differently. I work with what someone once called "mathematical idealities," with the emphasis firmly placed on the second word—idealities—because it's really not about mathematics after all. It's not so much the words that I use, mystifying symbols to achieve my ends, but that given the opportunity to move forward in various ways, I opt for the faculty of performing abstractions and archetypes, for the faculty of imagining things. The first method thinks of the surface retroactively; I anticipate it. Here lies perhaps the only disagreement, but it's a really big one.

I have been talking about the surface for quite a bit already, and now is the time to maybe state a few reasons why. I like it, because it offers us practical and theoretical challenges analogous to the challenges of a traditional architectural discourse, with the difference that thinking about the surface is thinking about architecture by analogy.

And this analogy is productive, because it frees us from making direct and automatic assumptions. We don't have to worry, for instance, about what things look like, or what they're supposed to look like. It's enough to focus on what they actually do.

Exploring this topic is for me primarily a problem of notation, and for some time now I've chosen to approach it almost exclusively in writing. By writing, I don't only mean writing a text, but approaching it through symbols and marks rather than figures and images. Now, since writing typically takes place on the surface of the page, writing involves surface as both subject matter and material support. We write about the surface on the surface, if you like, and thinking of the variable surface as both means and end of that performance of writing leads us to metonymic shifts with rich implications on the formulation of concepts.

When it comes to creating new surfaces, writing of course takes a completely different role altogether. It implies a different recourse to generative symbols and marks. This is about using symbolic equations rather than ordinary software or surface software, or symbols rather than buttons and sliders. Working in this manner today requires a Zen-like mindset. We live in an age of immediacy, super software, smooth person-machine interfaces, and working with parametric equations, as my students and I do, means choosing the arid discipline of writing over the futile pleasures of modeling.

The process of parametric generation produces a continuous surface made of lines, of threads. The truth is that the surface of discrete mathematics and computation does not exist. In fact, we only have lines or threads; hence, the transition to materiality is usually quite straightforward. If the lines are two-dimensional, we can use them to turn centerlines for parallel laser-cut material profiles. If the threads are now two-dimensional, we can use them to print doubly curved members, and the threads are effectively laminated from the ground up.

My point is that materiality does not only begin with matter. The possibility of producing material undercuts, recesses, self-intersections, holes, and other signs of formal complexity is linked to the mathematical model's ability to describe variation—and, critically, to our own willingness to qualify it conceptually.

Consider for instance the impressive medium of rapid prototyping. Unlike the laser cutter, its technically inferior counterpart, the 1:1 correspondence rapid prototyping draws between data and physical artifact eliminates the need for tectonics. But is that good or bad? Building without tectonics is a dull proposition in the best of times, so we are certainly entitled to ask: is rapid prototyping primitive? Is laser cutting advanced? Both systems do one thing really well. As you've probably figured by now, I love splitting hairs about instruments, because deep down, and even on the surface, their limitations reflect our own.

Experiments in Tessellation: The Airport Terminal

Farshid Moussavi

Options Studio, Spring 2008 **Teaching Associate:** Daniel López-Pérez. **Students:** Heather Boesch, Shin Hyung Cho, Ryan Culligan, Katherine Foreman, Michael Harris, Lee Huang, Soe Won Hwang, David Jaubert, Mathieu Lemieux Blanchard, Jungmin Nam, Soojung Rhee, Ivan Shumkov, Lukas Thorn. **Catia Instruction:** Jordan Brandt. **Participants:** Hanif Kara, Lluis Ortega.

Airport terminals are essentially "sheds"—large volumes of space, with long spans and no major subdivisions, to cater to the flows of people and goods that they enclose. The shed can be regarded as an "abstract machine," a versatile idea that has accommodated a wide range of functions from train stations to museums. Though a variety of structural solutions have been developed for the shed, producing a variety of forms, the shed has remained a modular system of growth, catering to repetitive organizations.

The fourth generation of airport terminals is currently producing larger sheds than ever before. China alone will build forty-eight new large airports in the next five years. These airport terminals are continuous building sites as they constantly expand to cater to larger aircraft; change and expansion is therefore adding an unprecedented level of complexity to the shed. Meanwhile, the airport terminal is required to act as a landmark, making the expression of the shed equally as important as its function. The new super-sized airport shed needs to be infinitely flexible and exceedingly unique.

Unlike the simple repetition of modules in conventional sheds, the studio explored tessellation as a part-whole system that allows for complex repetition through an aggregation of diverse parts. The complexity of this repetition is a function of the degree of correspondence built into the part-to-whole relationship. The studio produced generative base units for the airport terminal that interrelated several components through a specific and common criteria—a plane of correspondence. This involved infusing the base unit with a particular mode of subjectivity that would, in parallel to the system of growth, breed unique traits of expression and affective qualities. Tessellation can involve variation as a consistent expressive trait of the base unit that generates variety and uniqueness as a consistent character of the system.

The studio tested these ideas at Shenzhen Bao'an International Airport in China, which plans to build a new terminal in two phases. The semester involved analyzing recent airport terminals as well as different large-span shed typologies that may be applicable to the airport terminal. The studio developed base units with specific protogeometries that could direct the growth of the super-shed. Primary organizational material—such as structure, circulation, natural lighting, and facade systems—was set in correspondence to produce novel configurations that can grow in a number of different ways in time.

Interior, Domestic Departures

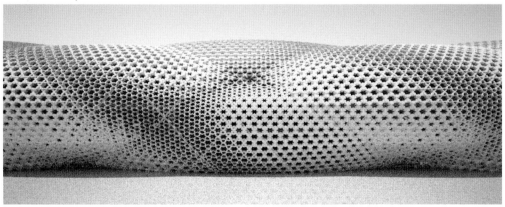

Elevation, International Departures

Michael Harris

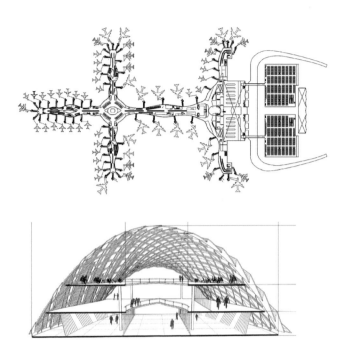

Ryan Culligan

Lukas Thorn

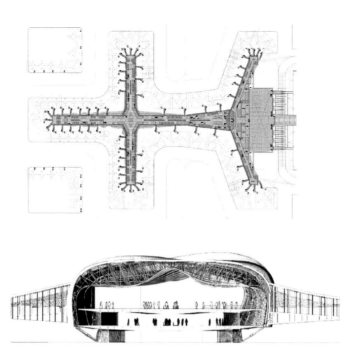

Mathieu Lemieux Blanchard

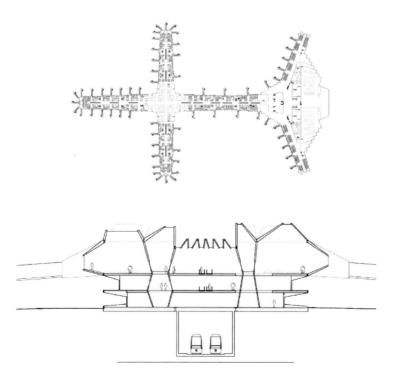

Soe Won Hwang

Ribbed dome   Aggregation of hexagonal domes   Plan of concourse

Katherine Foreman

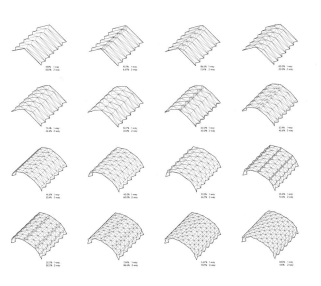

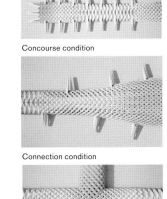

Concourse condition

Connection condition

Cross condition

Transitional sections

Super Tall:
Performance and Atmosphere

Hani Rashid

Options Studio, Fall 2007 Teaching Associate: Theo Sarantoglou Lalis. **Students:** Garrick Ambrose, Brigid Boyle, Lior Galili, Elie Gamburg, Andrei Gheorghe, Frederick Ortner, Trevor Patt, Veronica Siebert, Gregory Spaw, Ina Chun Yee Wong, Hyuck Jin Yoon, Sandra Cyin Yum. **Research Assistant:** Christopher Johnson

The intent of the studio was to seek out architectural strategies (rooted in digital media) that are preoccupied with "performance," and through such research, the building design that achieves elegance and control within intense urban contexts. The focus of the studio was "super tall" buildings—those that climb beyond 400 meters in height.

The studio explored the notion of performance in architecture as it relates to the use and manipulation of digital processes, new materials and materiality, non-standardization processes, urban intervention, and the notion of vertical urbanism. The goal of the studio was to redefine what constitutes performance in this genre of architecture, and to formulate a way of designing and describing such architecture as having more to do with atmosphere and effect than with form and structure.

Key areas of studio research included:

Urban Intervention: Cities from Las Vegas to Kuala Lumpur are seeking out and vying for super tall buildings as indicators of economic strength and as placeholders for future growth and potential. Each city chosen was viewed for its cultural nuances and distinction rather than its tradition and symbolism. Notions of vertical urbanism were key to understanding the role of these buildings in such contemporary urban situations.

Technology and Image: Utilization of computer aided tools and software to configure and develop design iterations for tall structures. The goal of this part of the studio was to achieve elegance and sophistication in the design studies, and to be able to comprehend and describe architecture in terms of its atmospheric condition and spatial effects.

Viability: Through a survey of new materials, methodologies, and advancements in engineering capabilities, students were encouraged to explore and push the limits of making such projects viable and realizable.

Pertinence: Development and clarity of understanding such structures in terms of environmental sustainability, energy consumption, and zero carbon aspirations.

Resonance and Response: Projects were assessed for their ability to produce atmospheric influences, thematic overlays, and iconic possibilities, raising questions about architecture as an instigator of meaning and desire.

Garrick Ambrose

Ina Wong, Hyuck Jin Yoon, Sandra Yum

Gregory Spaw

Frederick Ortner

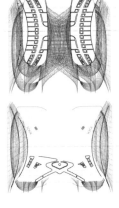

Elie Gamburg

Andrei Gheorghe

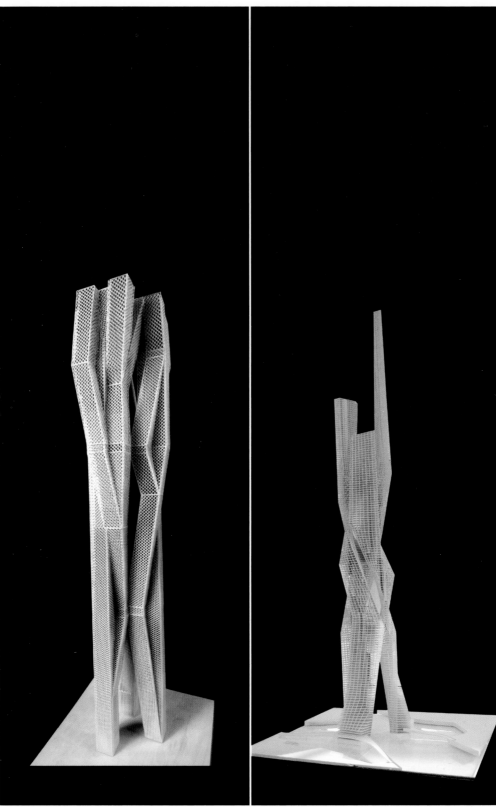

Garrick Ambrose

Ina Wong, Hyuck Jin Yoon, Sandra Yum

Gregory Spaw   **Frederick Ortner**

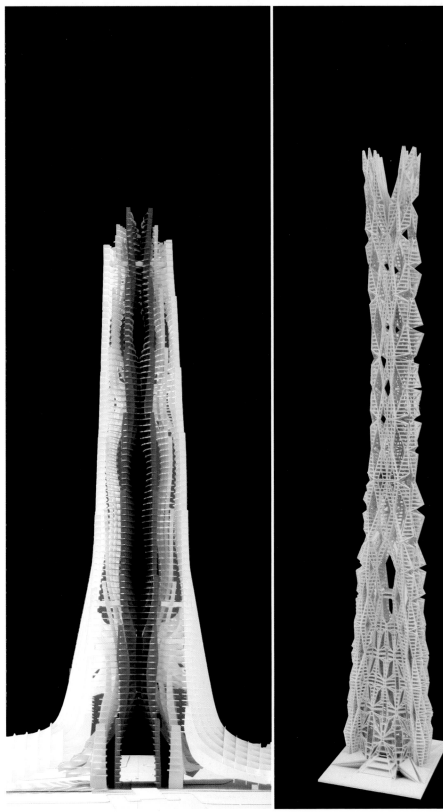

Elie Gamburg

Andrei Gheorge

The Grid as an Organizational Device for the Design of the City

Joan Busquets, Felipe Correa
Seminar, Fall 2007 **Students:** Maria Josefa Arquero de Alarcon, Carlos Cabrera, Danielle Choi, Benjamin Fortunato, Elie Gamburg, Patrick Hobgood, Ming-Jen Hsueh, Ioannis Kandyliaris, Manuel Lap Yan Lam, Cheng-Yang Lee, Athina Loumou, Isaiah Miller, Yu Morishita, Ilias Papageorgiou, David Pearson, Robyn Perkins, Zhenqing Que, Seetha Raghupathy, Christoforos Romanos, Dong Woo Yim, Da-Un Yoo, Yingfan Zhang. **Teaching Assistant:** Maria Josefa Arquero de Alarcon.

Current fast-paced forms of urbanization demand new spatial configurations conceived with more flexible and open-ended systems that can accommodate diverse speeds of urban growth. These new urban scenarios favor loose, yet efficient organizational mechanisms that can accommodate diversity and change while proffering extensive city densification and expansion. Within this framework, the value and metrics of the urban grid are more operative today than ever. A reinterpretation of the role of "the grid" in the contemporary constructed environment can serve as an essential tool to rethink the restructuring of existing urban fragments, as well as to project new forms of densification.

The research seminar focused on the investigation and evaluation of urbanist projects which use grid systems as their main organizational and structural device. The ultimate objective of the research is to spawn a new understanding of the possibilities that emerge from the urban grid, and to capitalize on the potential transformations of latticed structures into inventive urban assembly models.

The research tackled six specific lines of inquiry:

Configurative Models: Diversity of grid layouts.

Morphological Features: The metrics and geometries of the grid.

Cultural Specifications: The molding of the grid through ideological frameworks.

Historical Transformations: Critical shifts in the organization of the grid.

Geographical Pressures: The role of environmental morphologies.

Adaptive Uses: The grid, its utilization, and how it affects geometry.

The outcome of this research, explored through diverse academic conduits (research seminars, independent studies, and studios) is expected to generate a significant body of work that presents the reinterpretation of the grid as a powerful tool for the design of the city.

New York, NY **United States**	**Buenos Aires** **Argentina**	**Cairo, IL** **United States**	**Taichung** **Taiwan**
Continuous / Uniform	Continuous / Uniform	Continuous / Uniform	Continuous / Subdivided

Base module

Intersection
hierarchy

Urban
section

Grid
hierarchy

Intersection
geometry

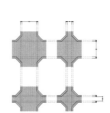
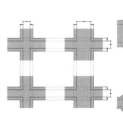
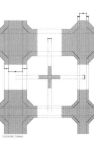

Carlos Cabrera, Elie Gamburg, David Pearson

Savannah, GA **United States**	**Lisbon** **Portugal**	**Edinburgh** **United Kingdom**	**Chennai** **India**
Continuous / Subdivided	Continuous / Subdivided	Discontinuous / Subdivided	Discontinuous / Non-Uniform

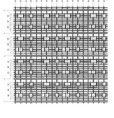 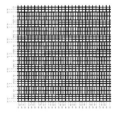  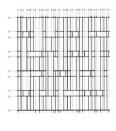

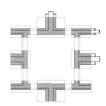 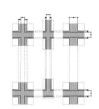 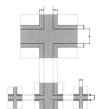

San Francisco, CA
United States

Continuous / Uniform

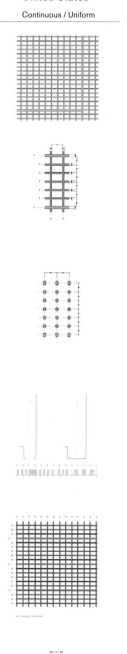

Base module

Intersection
hierarchy

Urban section

Grid hierarchy

Intersection
geometry

Case 1

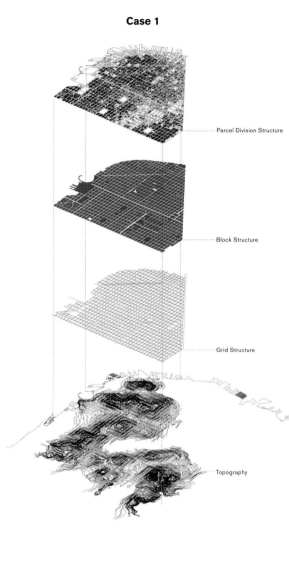

Parcel Division Structure

Block Structure

Grid Structure

Topography

Case 2

Case 3

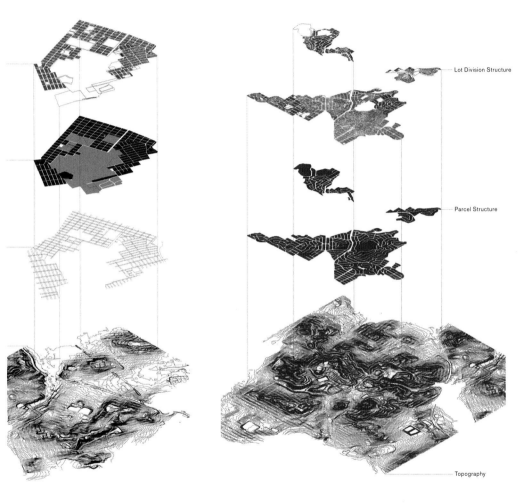

Lot Division Structure

Parcel Structure

Topography

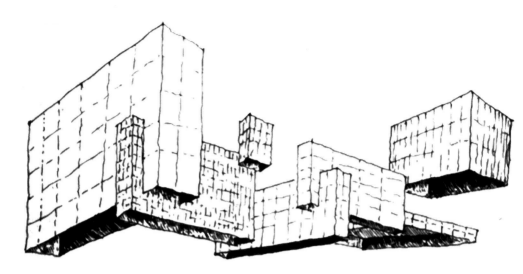

What exactly is a superblock? It's precisely the term's elusive quality that renders it at once terrifically appealing and terribly perilous. The OED lists the first published usage of the term as occurring in 1928, in reference to Clarence Stein and Henry Wright's urban project for Radburn, New Jersey. As envisioned, Radburn's superblocks were described in the press as extra large Manhattan blocks: "take a New York city block… and pump ambition to lead a better life into it until it expands to ten or fifteen times its present area—say till it measures over a thousand feet on one side and nearly two thousand on the other."

With this single, short description the paradox underlying the superblock reveals itself. While decidedly urban in its terminology, the word "superblock" originated with a suburban plan that looked more to Ebenezer Howard and Raymond Unwin's Garden City movement than to Manhattan for its inspiration.

In his article of 1971, "The Superblock," architectural historian Alan Colquhoun defines the superblock in economic terms, explaining that it consists of "large pieces of real

estate, each of which is financed and organized as a single entity." Colquhoun under-scores that there is no consistent formal characteristic qualifying the superblock: "The size of each unit… is not determined by any single physical factor….
But however individual cases may differ, there is always one common factor: the enor-mous reserves of capital that exist in the modern economy which enable either private or public agencies, or a combination of both, to gain control over, and make a profit from, ever larger areas of urban land."

Colquhoun's definition rings familiar with a more generalized critique of the postwar city that focused particularly on the ties between urban development and capital. Jean-Luc Godard's 1967 film, *2 ou 3 choses que je sais d'elle*, contrasts lively street scenes in the older sections of Paris, shot from a walking person's perspective, with desolate aerial views of the recently constructed urban landscape of low horizontal slabs on plinths—all housing—that underscore the anonymity of the more modern Parisian metroscape. Throughout the movie, a foreboding voice-over elides capitalism with urban anonymity and state control, underscoring the point that it is the govern-ment that harbors control over the city's superblocks of land and money. If the film's urban landscape shares some similarities with scenes of American urban renewal, however, Godard's voice-over cannot be applied to the American example; unlike France or the rest of Europe, in the United States, governmental policies had more ramifications on the suburban than the urban landscape.

At the same time, however, in the postwar period "ever larger areas of urban land" did get developed in the United States. These large urban insertions offer a differ-ent model of the superblock than their European counterparts; rather than being the product of governmental policies, these superblocks included housing, but were also seats of institutions: universities, hospitals, and other large scale entities that allied themselves with business, the community, and with other institutions in order to redefine the postwar American city. Rather than following the isolationist model of suburban superblock planning like Radburn, these decidedly urban superblocks were extroverted and permeable, both formally and administratively. This moment of post-war reflection in the United States led to certain innovations in both architecture and urbanism and resulted in a new form of public subjectivity. The confluence of munici-pal politics, capital, and institutional agency established the genetic code for mid-century American urban dynamics, and this code may still provide fodder for some of today's urgent questions, especially in urbanism, and especially at the super-scale.

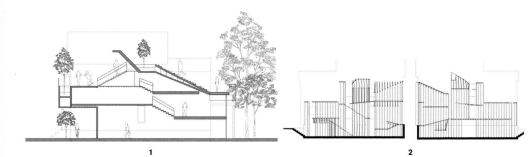

1

2

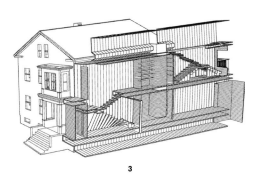

3

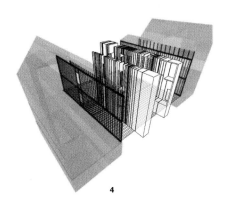

4

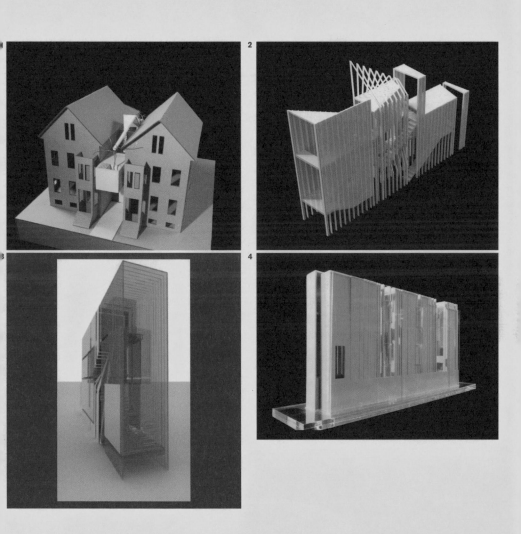

Core I Architecture, Fall 2007
Project 2: Double Door

1 Ghazal Abbasy Asbagh **2** Alda Black

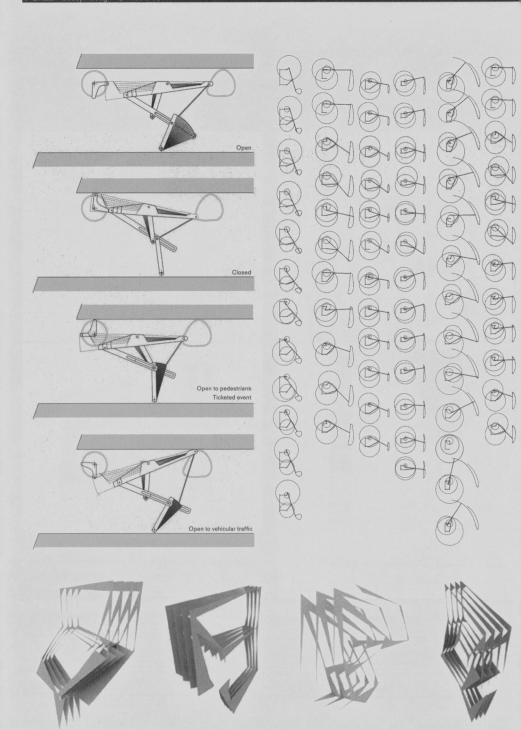

Open

Closed

Open to pedestrians
Ticketed event

Open to vehicular traffic

Core I Architecture, Fall 2007

Project 3: Triple Dormer

1 Eli Allen   **2** Theodore Baab   **3** Patricia Ebner   **4** Jennifer French

1

2

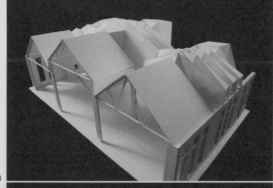

3

4

Thesis, Spring 2008
Smooth City: Reinhabiting Chicago's West Loop
Daniel Spiegel

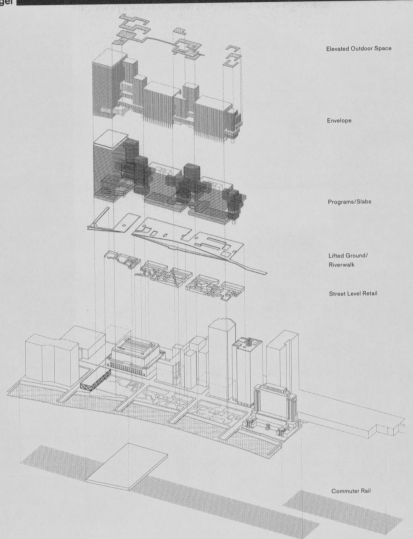

Elevated Outdoor Space

Envelope

Programs/Slabs

Lifted Ground/
Riverwalk

Street Level Retail

Commuter Rail

Exploded axonometric of project layers

Perspective view from riverside

Thesis, Spring 2008

GreyMatters: Differential Surface Interactions

Joshua Dannenberg

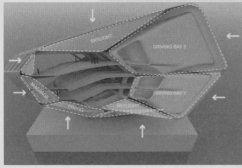

Module analysis

Building section

Aerial view of runway precinct and driving range

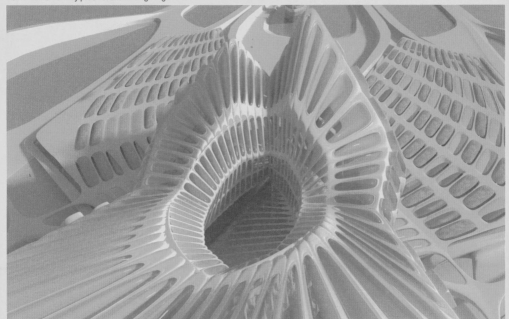

View of driving range

Nature

Excerpt: What Is Life?
Sanford Kwinter
Lecture, May 30, 2008

I have been secretly waiting for some journalist or other inquirer to ask me what I imagine is the most important concept of the 20th century and to expound on what and why. This fantasy is already fifteen years old and no such question has come my way, and so allow me to ask the question myself and answer it. The answer I dreamed to give is: "the concept of the chreod, of course!"

The what?

The chreod. The concept of the chreod was invented by one of the great and most fertile biological minds of the 20th century, Conrad Hal Waddington. Waddington's importance is inestimable, both as biologist and as a philosopher of the life sciences. Waddington had a penchant for mathematical and geometric modeling to organize and explain biological processes, and in this he either himself invented, or caused to be invented, some of the most profound intellectual models in the history of science. Among these was the branch of topology known as catastrophe theory and his own model of epigenetic development and the concept of the chreod.

A chreod—even the name was invented; it is a combination of the Greek words for determined or necessary and pathway—belongs to a theory of formation in which space is deeply implicated both in its genesis and its product. It refers to an invisible but not imaginary feature in an invisible but not imaginary landscape on which

a developing form gathers the information and the influence necessary for it to make itself what it is. Forms develop on such virtual landscapes not simply because they need a way to determine what they should look like and how they should behave, but because all forms are products of forces in the world that require resolution. The chreod explains how forces can come to become embedded in forms. The landscape or surface on which they develop is a model that allows multiple forces to engage one another, to integrate and to produce geometrical, chemical, and physical moduluses.

To understand the concept of the chreod one must first accept the premise that forces organize within, and give shape to virtual landscapes that then serve as the molds or templates for form development. These landscapes to which I am refer-ring are of course just models—essentially mathematical or topological models—even though they can also be actual landscapes too, as in the case of our Pleistocene savannahs in which the human form was forged out of an ape form.

A chreod is a topographical feature on this landscape that controls or constrains the movement of a developing form as it moves through it. It is easiest to think of chreods as basins of varying shape that direct the flow of matter, just as gravity in an Alpine valley would channel the runoff of melting snow. The actual path that a drop of water takes, would determine its precise and individual form. But the larger parameters of what path it could take are very highly constrained. Every form somehow incorporates the limits of the chreod in which it forms.

It is very important not to think of chreods as fixed molds or templates but rather as *pathways*. Chreods capture and channel forces and direct them to interact with matter over time. They do not rigidly determine forms, but simply direct, constrain, and protect their development. Every form reflects and resembles the chreod in which it took form, yet no form is ever a direct copy of the chreod that produced it. The chreod contributes both the general plan to the form but also, given the fact that it is a highly oriented landscape feature such as a steep incline, the compulsion to become form.

So what is it that makes the chreod such an important concept? First, it is the postu-late that there exists a matrix space that would underlie concrete forms, and which is formal itself. For example, it is well accepted that the broader landscape of which the chreod is but a single feature, and which is known technically as an epigenetic land-scape, is itself largely determined by genetic information and instructions. In other words, code has its place in the living shape system, and contributes significantly to the form. But code at best generates tendencies, parameters, and each of its inputs is tempered and modified by its interaction with other inputs from the code level; the landscape it produces is a product of all the interactions of inputs from the code, and these interactions are non-linear which means that their outcome is not necessarily knowable in advance or even entirely anticipatable. The bottom line: code generates developmental landscapes, NOT forms themselves.

The second thing that makes chreods important is the idea that there is a coherent system of tensions that determine the development of form and that can in turn be read or intuited in the form itself. This aspect has two important consequences. The first is that the profuse variety and individuality of forms maintains its stability and legibility by means of tethers that make the underlying chreods intuitable, a bit like one intuits the key in which a musical composition is written by deducing it from the constraints on the selection of notes in the song. This allows one to recognize same-ness even in the face of novelty and irreducible difference. For example, think back to the early and mid-90s, when computer typographics was developing very quickly and certain, especially West Coast graphic designers began to use distressed and eroded fonts that were barely legible. But the legibility of the text field was strategi-cally preserved anyway, largely by calling up cognitive competences on the part of the reader that were essentially chreodic: one no longer read the forms themselves but one read through the wreckage of letterforms to the matrix of chreodic tensions that produce a "5" or an "and" in the first place.

The second consequence has to do with the idea of kinship. Chreods establish the possibility of families of forms and of relationships of forms. When Goethe famously took his walks through the German forests to gather and to contemplate plants he was reflecting on their embedded formal logic. His search for the *Urpflanze* (or the originary plant) was not a literal search for something that would fill a speci-men bag, but a search for the pure chreodic shape from which the plethora of plants represent variations. In the present case of plants, the chreod is expressable both as a drawing/diagram or as an algorithm. You will find both if you read Goethe's book called *The Metamorphosis of Plants*. Among the more astonishing and notable aspects of his analysis is to have intuited, and made analytically explicit, the interac-tions of several superimposed movements, and through a wide variety of different parameters and combinations. All told, there were three fundamental gradients (you could call these dimensions) of which every plant, and every part of every plant repre-sented one point in the 3-D space of interactions or possibilities. To see chreods is to see and think in phase space (or "possibility space").

This brings us to the third thing that makes chreods so important: chreods are complex, mollusk-like sections cut through a "motor space" or a motor field. In other words, chreods depict sections of *development*, not static shapes; they are figures of time. A chreod tells you the general parameters that a shape will take on, which are fully specific without needing to be exact. A person's smile for example—a paroxysm that happens to the face—changes from the age of six months to the age of forty; it does not however abandon its regulating chreod and so remains recognizable as a stable identity despite the manifold transformations that a given face might undergo over time. It is a famous assertion in neuropsychology that humans can tell the difference between a real and a fake smile (different motors —muscles and pulleys— are used to produce it). Chreods are motion templates: they are the geometrical equivalent and translation of algorithms.

Ecology.Synergy.Design

Behnisch Architekten, Transsolar Climate Engineering
Exhibition, August 22–October 3, 2007 Curator: Frank Ockert, FMO, Stuttgart. **Collaborators:** IFA; German Institute for Foreign Cultural Relations represented by the Goethe Institute; Galerie Aedes, Berlin.

The exhibition addressed the widespread and misleading quantitative interpretation of the term "sustainability" by highlighting the manifold aspects of sustainability that constitute important qualities in themselves. Selected projects by Behnisch Architekte and Transsolar Climate Engineering were presented to illustrate their working method: the results of their previous collaborations, and perspectives for the future. The exhibition was aimed not only at architects and engineers, but at all those who care about the quality of the built environment and its impact, from school children to political, scientific, and economic decision-makers. Rather than present models for a sustainab architecture, the exhibition provoked a redefinition of the term "sustainability" by drawing on the five human senses, to focus on the complex series of relationships between human beings and their immediate environment.

Behnisch Architekten and Transsolar Climate Engineering have collaborated for years in pursuit of an environmentally responsive architecture. Works extend from architectural competitions to large-scale realized projects, both in Germany and abroad. Current common projects include Harvard's Allston Science Complex in Cambridge, M Senscity Paradise Universe in Las Vegas, NV; Thermal Baths in Bad Aibling, Germany and the Arizona State University Gateway Project in Tempe, AZ. Their collaborative design approach is founded on the shared belief that high-quality built environments can be achieved through the responsible use of natural resources. Curiosity, commodit and delight drive an innovative process combining technical advancements with passi design measures.

The following is a response to a questionnaire originally given to Charles Eames and titled "What Is Design?" on the occasion of an exhibition of the same name at the Musee d'Orsay in Paris in 1969. The questions were re-posed to Erwan Bouroullec by Michael Meredith and Lluís Ortega on the occasion of his lecture at the GSD on October 17, 2007.

What is your definition of "design?"

Using a certain kind of ingenuity (or creative force) to give a "shape" (a full DNA) to everyday objects and furnitures.

Is design an expression of art (an art form)?

Design is here to shape part of our surroundings. As a result, it takes part in our way of standing in the world. So it has certain art values.

Is design a craft for industrial purposes?

Considering that my main tool is a pen and a sketchbook, I would say so.

What are the boundaries of design?

Culture, to be understood as the knowledge that makes people behave "properly" within a situation or a specific context. There are cultural boundaries linked to the adequation of objects to a precise context and use.

Is design a discipline that concerns itself with only one part of the environment?

Through work, we concentrate and focus on subjects that don't interest people in detail, but rather aim at general audiences.

It is a method of general expression?

It can be a way of behaving in the world. But to be honest, design is rather polite (in the sense that it is restricted to a limited amount of objects), and this is not enough to make a mankind.

Is design a creation of an individual? ... Or a creation of a group?

Design is a place where certain group intuitions take place in individual creation, and vice-versa.

Is there a design ethic?

Hopefully there are many design ethics.

Does design imply the idea of products that are necessarily useful?

For my own definition: YES, but with an understanding of "useful" that is deep and vast enough.

It is able to cooperate in the creation of works reserved solely for pleasure?

Pleasure is a sign of wellness, which design has a lot to do with.

Ought form to derive from the analysis of function?

Form ought to derive from the analysis of the understanding (the culture) one has of a function.

Can the computer substitute for the designer?

If only a computer could drive a car, or prepare a decent coffee, we could try some further steps.

Does design imply industrial manufacture?

No. Why should it be always so?

Is design an element of industrial policy?

It is always a subject that lies within any industry. Some have a clever understanding of it, and usually it provokes a better result.

Ought design to care about lowering costs?

Quite often yes, but it should never always be the case.

Does the creation of design admit constraint?

Design cannot accept any point in which a constraint cannot be answered through a fair dialogue.

What constraints?

The most important are the ones resulting from the understanding of the culture of the user.

Does design obey laws?

There are many of them, and I can never remind myself of all of them at once. Many rules are contextual, when some are absolute. Justness is very important.

Ought the final product to bear the trademark of the designer? Of the research office?

Why not? Should we print books without authors?

What is the relation of design to the world of fashion (current trends)?

We operate on very different time frames, so there are a lot of misunderstandings between the two. Everything seems to change very fast. At the same time, some deeper moves reveal themselves after longer periods of time, like fifty or sixty years. It is important not only to pay attention to surface changes, but rather to follow a deeper intuition.

Is design ephemeral?

Unfortunately, no; fortunately, yes.

Ought it to tend towards the ephemeral or towards permanence?

When a project tends to permanence, then something really strong has been achieved. The concept of ephemeral is quite relative. Compared to fashion, for example, even ephemeral objects seem to last longer.

To whom does design address itself: to the greatest number (the masses)? To the specialists or the enlightened amateur? To a privileged social class?

The idea to work for the greatest number is exciting, which includes all the people you describe. The creation process does not always focus on the "kind of customer," but rather on the people that will use an object.

Can public action aid the advancement of design?

A few private companies have been so brave and modern that we have earned respect for them. In a sense, one can even think that some have been assumed a public role. But of course public action has often helped us cross the boundaries that the consumer market may create.

After having answered all these questions, do you feel you have been able to practice the profession of "design" under satisfactory conditions, or even optimum conditions?

I would say so, also considering that with time we became more and more thrilled by the enormous goals that design might achieve within its own field.

Have you been forced to accept compromises?

I don't feel so, but time might bring us a different understanding.

What do you feel is the primary condition for the practice of design, and its propagation?

An understanding of its real necessity.

What is the future of design?

Its own future. By which I mean: design has ever, and will always exist.

Algae

Clips

Rock

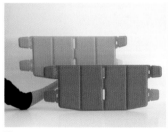

Tiles

Natural and Urban, Green and Grey?
Studies on Specifications of Contemporary Urban Architecture
Inès Lamunière, Options Studio, Spring 2008 **Teaching Associate:** Roberto de Oliveira Castro. **Students:** Abdulatif Almishari, Ryan Bollom, Ricardo Camacho, Hoi Lung Chan, Vivian Chan, Aude-Line Duliere, Maciej Kaczynski, Patricia Sakata, Clara Wong. **Participant:** Patrick Devanthéry.

The city is everywhere; the city is nowhere. What project for that difficult city? In what terms can the architecture of buildings construct the city and question its urban planning? How do new lifestyles and different types of mobility change our perception of urban space? How can the evolution of technologies linked to energy resources renew construction and its expression in the urban fabric? In what circumstances are private and public space blurred? How can density become a quality? Can a new relationship be found between nature and artifice, "urban" figure and "natural" ground, inside and outside? These are some of the questions addressing the architectural project of the 21st-century city.

The studio project was a pretext to explore the specificity of urban character in architecture today. It was located in the gentrified Chelsea district of Manhattan, with a program of mixed activities including housing, retail, offices, publicly accessible functions, and an elevated slow-mobility infrastructure. Throughout the semester, programs evolved and defined themselves around the idea of mixed use and flexibility in urban structure and fabric.

The studio project was also a pretext to explore the "unreasonable" urban need for nature, or at least the idea of "natural" things: natural light, air, materials, vegetation ... A warm sun, a cold fog, a rainy storm, a refreshing wind on a hot day, a shadow in the strong light, wet or dry climates, sunny or dark atmospheres; the smell of rain on the sidewalk, the perfume of humid grass, the color of orchids, and the generic green of domestic plants ... Each project was an opportunity to redefine the relationship to nature on a physiological basis, and in terms of a sustainable development of our environment.

The studio developed a large mixed-use building in which residential program was redefined to create a dialogue with nature, as an inescapable artifact of the 21st century. Architectural projects were used to invent a particular relationship between urban shelter, density, climate, and anatomy, and elaborated new living conditions concentrating on the atmospheric qualities of contemporary construction (materials and fabrics, but also ventilation, temperature, light, and humidity), to create a sense of "green" from the body to the city block.

Abdulatif Almishari

Ryan Bollom

Clara Wong

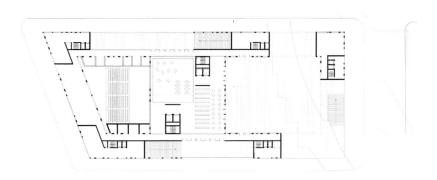

Abdulatif Almishari

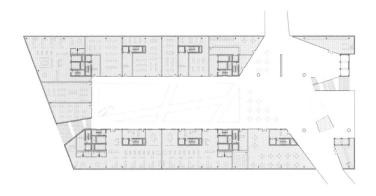

Ryan Bollom

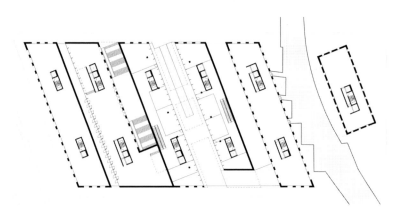

Clara Wong

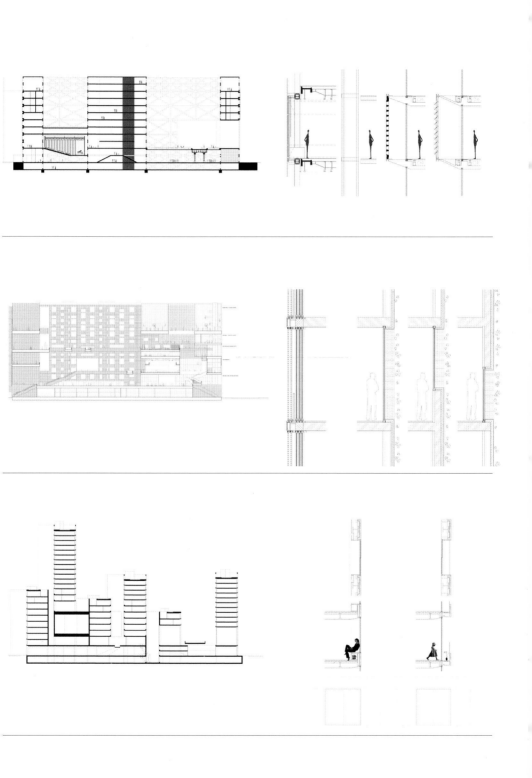

Excerpt: The Nature of Green in the Yellow Landscapes of Bahrain

Gareth Doherty
DDes Essay, 2008

As a color, green does not exist by itself: it is a mix of blue and yellow. Colors have subjective boundaries, and where blue becomes green or green becomes yellow depends to a large extent on the culture and background of the perceiver, as well as on light, time of day, the material, and context. In 1969, the anthropologists Brent Berlin and Paul Kay described the relativity of color across languages, writing that a word for green almost always exists even when a word for blue does not.[1]

Green also needs water. Where water is in short supply, the potency of green becomes much greater. Although frequently considered an antidote to the urban, in arid environments greenery often indicates the presence of human settlements, since both require water. Perceptions of what is urban can change over time: picturesque villages which were once considered urban could be considered pastoral and rural today. As the locus and scale of commerce has and population density shifts, so too can perceptions of what is urban, and indeed of what is green. Urban and green are not opposites; in fact they are organizationally similar and require similar infrastructures. Green today is more than a color, or vegetation, or open space. It is a type of building or urbanism, an environmental cause, a political movement. Green is an urban condition, requiring not just a complex infrastructure to support it but one that has a value for society too.

With its hot arid climate, the indigenous landscapes of the Persian/Arabian Gulf are mostly shades of yellow and brown and, apart from the odd oasis, are especially devoid of green. Before desalination and treated sewage effluent became the norm for maintaining green space, Bahrain's greenness was due mainly to the plethora of underground and underwater springs that give Bahrain its name.[2] Together, water and greenery created what was perceived as life-giving produce and beauty. The saying "Water, Greenery, and a Beautiful Face" (Al-maa wa al-houdra wa al-wajh al-hasan) reminds us that these are three very good things—all that one could want. This popular saying, which is most probably pre-Islamic, indicates that green has a long and deep cultural significance in the Arab world.

The groves of green-gray date palms that used to cover the north and west coasts of Bahrain are without doubt the country's most iconic and distinctive green spaces. Writing about the social life of the date palms, Faud Khuri states that the culture of palms in Bahrain was as elaborate and highly developed as the culture of camels among the pastoral nomads in central Arabia.[3] Supposedly it was not uncommon for farmers in Bahrain to give their trees names, like children, and in this way treat them as family members. The date palm gardens are important spaces with a productive past: every part of the date is edible, and until relatively recently dates were a staple food in Bahrain. The dates, the leaves, the trunk all had a particular use: in this sense, the date palm was urban, penetrating all aspects of Bahraini life and providing food, shelter, social spaces, and social status.

While the date palm groves were sources of both food and employment for the working classes, they were also recreation grounds for the elite. Owning land in Bahrain had, and still has, complex social meanings and overloads. Large date palm plantations were owned by city merchants who invested in them not for their income but for the status such ownership conferred.[4] The ability to retreat to the groves was the preserve of the elite. Wealthy merchants would bring their families to the palm groves on Friday afternoons and would issue invitations to relatives and friends to join them there. Visiting cards, to be presented at the gate, would sometimes be issued to friends to grant them permission to visit in the absence of the owner.

Green residential compounds that exist today in Bahrain, such as Green Oasis on the Budaiya Highway, are in partial compensation for the date palm groves that they replace. Together with the date palms of roundabouts, roadside edges, and median strips of VIP roads (designed for verdant greenery but also with issues of security in mind), they represent the green of contemporary Bahrain. Such infrastructural spaces are important because they constitute the greenery that most people encounter nowadays in everyday life in Bahrain. They do not so much represent the past—though the palm trees do make reference to this past—as they speak of Bahrain's present, its place in the world, and its aspirations for the future. The roadside spaces of Bahrain have a strange but important social value. Take the area adjacent to the Pearl Roundabout, a central traffic interchange. On weekends and in the evenings it is not unusual to see expatriates sitting along the roadside quite comfortably having picnics and either savoring or ignoring the high-speed traffic alongside. Though it is primarily an infrastructural space, its green still retains some of its social value.

The date palm gardens and the traffic spaces of the city are not so much contrasting opposites but have similar types of social values. These roadside greenery spaces are, in a way, the date palm groves of the present, representing the power of the state through the transformation of the desert. Both have a certain type of production, though these productive qualities are obviously different: the palm groves are agricultural and social, whereas the green roadsides indicate an economic productivity, a production of development—a landscape of transformation. The plethora of green roundabouts and median strips, lined with petunias in the national colors of red and white, betray this contemporary understanding of development.

Water, like blue, is fundamental to green. And water is in short supply in the Gulf: arguably no issue is more important for national security in the Gulf region than the availability of water. Greenery is a major consumer of national water quotas and a single date palm requires up to 200 liters of water per day. When factoring in the costs of water—environmental as well as financial—greenery is, not surprisingly, exceedingly expensive to maintain.

Advertising and global positioning have become new infrastructures of green. The representation of green though future projects can transport the viewer to other worlds, creating fractured geographies, sites that echo far-away places. "It's like Scotland, minus the weather …" claims an advertisement for Riffa Views, a luscious green residential development built on top of the desert. These fractured geographies are largely responsible for the sense of fantasy in current Gulf urbanism. Advertising for new developments typically uses green to sell projects, sometimes with a higher percentage of the image given over to green spaces than to the building that is apparently for sale.

The transformative power of turning desert to green is an extremely potent one. To turn desert into luscious green is to achieve the impossible, to prove that dreams do become reality, to show that paradise can be constructed on earth. The anthropologist Maurice Bloch has written that to be effective, a transformation needs to be of a certain magnitude; turning desert into gravel or concrete is not as potent a transformation as turning desert into green.[5] But the presence of the desert cannot be forgotten: even in its absence, it is very much present.

Today, new meanings for green are being adopted in the English language. The environmental, ecological, and political aspects of green are becoming more apparent across the globe, and are beginning to be felt in the Gulf, albeit in a limited and particular way. A significant project is the Masdar development in Abu Dhabi, designed by Foster and Partners. Masdar, meaning "The Source" in Arabic, is being marketed as the world's first zero-carbon city. Cars are relegated underground, and the city will be powered through solar energy. The Amwaj Gateway project is claimed to be the first LEED-registered project in Bahrain despite the fact it is built on an artificial island.

The Arabic word for landscape, *manthar tabi'iyy*, literally translates as "natural scenery," an indicator that landscape is not just about how things look but also about their nature, their natural order, and the way they work. Green is part of a wider social, political, economic, ecological network. Perhaps we can learn from the palm groves themselves, where date palms share the land with rotational crops, fruit and vegetables, and the grazing of animals and fowl, and where water is rationed according to detailed customary laws. Perhaps a better future lies in the layering of spaces with multiple uses, in recognizing the various roles and meanings of green, in its infrastructures, and in more sensitively planning and designing for greenery in limited space like that of Bahrain.[6]

1 Brent Berlin and Paul Kay, *Basic Color Terms: Their Universality and Evolution* (Berkeley: University of California Press, 1969).
2 Bahrain means "two seas" in Arabic.
3 Faud Khuri, *Tribe and State Bahrain: The Transformation of Social and Political Authority in an Arab State* (Chicago: University of Chicago Press, 1980), p. 39.
4 It is important to note that the date palm gardens of the past—as with those of the present—were not always profitable. Indeed it was possible to make a living there, but the returns cannot have been great. One large property was sold in 1943 for 40,000 rupees (about $1.2 million in today's money), while a shop in the souq at that time cost about one tenth the price, at 4,000 rupees. This land was then rented out at a rate of 27.5 rupees a month on average, netting an annual rent of 330 rupees, or approximately 1 percent of the value of the property. This was not a good financial investment, and it is fair to deduce that the purchase must have been made for social prestige.
5 Maurice Bloch, "Why Trees, Too, are Good to Think With: Towards an Anthropology of the Meaning of Life," in Laura Rival, ed., *The Social Life of Trees* (New York: Berg Publishers, 1998).
6 Bahrain is extremely small and dense compared to other cities and city-states in the Arab world. There are roughly four square meters of green area per person in Bahrain; this compares favorably with Cairo, considered the city with the lowest percentage of green space in the world, which has a rate of approximately 1.6 square meters of green space per person. In contrast, Dubai has the ambition to have 23 meters of green per person by 2012. As one planner has stated, "why is it that Bahrain thinks it can be so different in getting by on less green space than Dubai?"

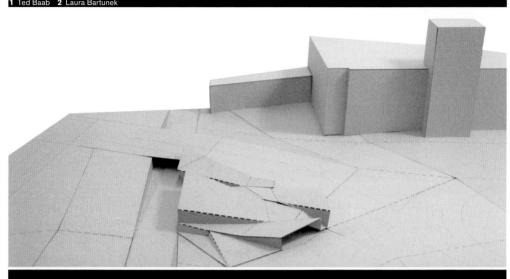

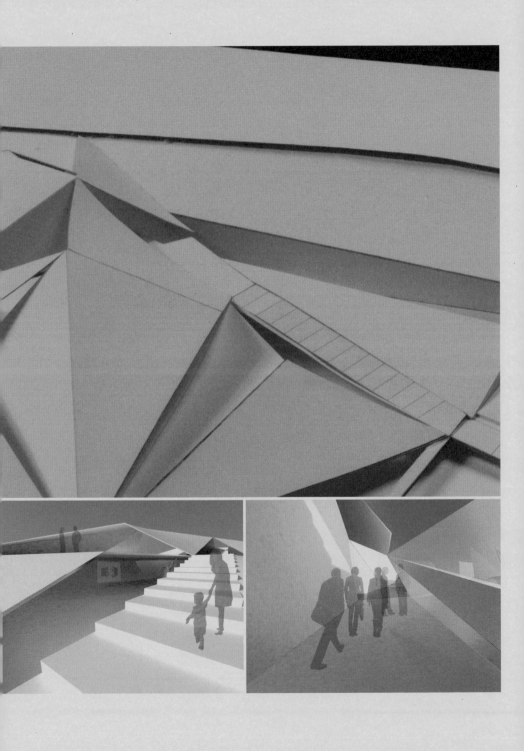

1 Shanshan Qi   **2** Joseph Bergen

Project 2: Allston Research Institute

3 Jeremiah Geiman   **4** Anna Protasevich

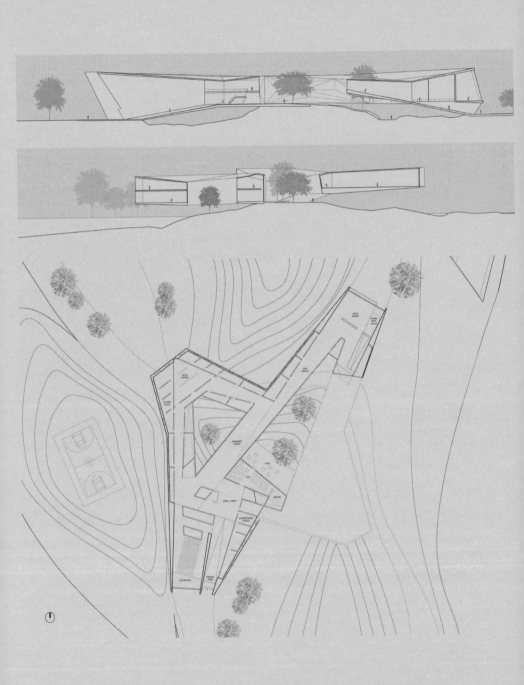

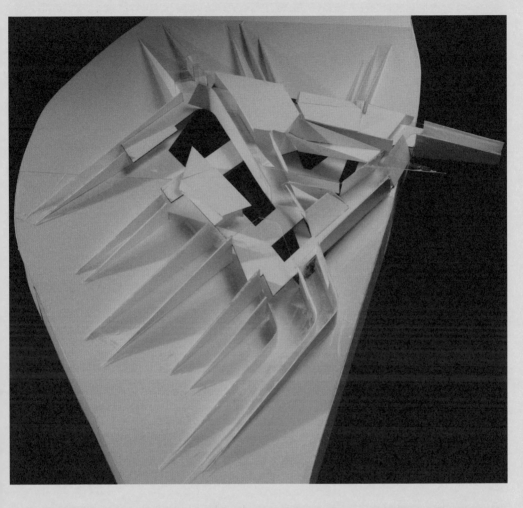

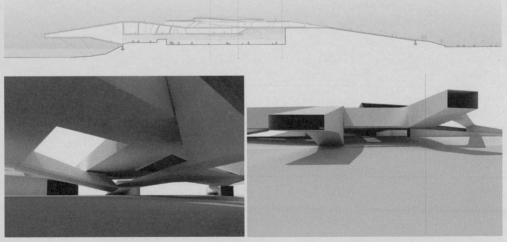

Thesis, Spring 2008
Avoiding Atlantis: Reconstituting Place in an Age of Global Warming
Sun-Young Park

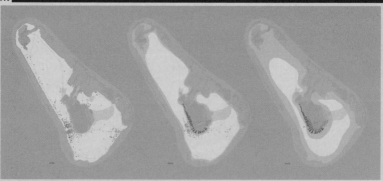

Vaitupu Lagoon Settlement Phasing

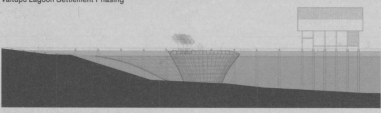

Vaitupu Lagoon "Bio-Rock" Foundation

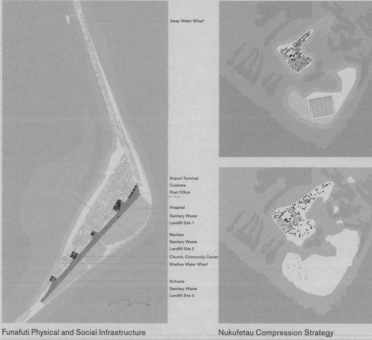

Deep Water Wharf

Airport Terminal
Customs
Post Office

Hospital
Sanitary Waste
Landfill Site 1

Markets
Sanitary Waste
Landfill Site 2

Church, Community Center
Shallow Water Wharf

Schools
Sanitary Waste
Landfill Site 3

Funafuti Physical and Social Infrastructure

Nukufetau Compression Strategy

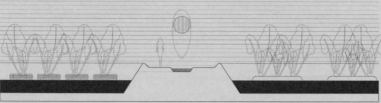

Nukufetau Pulaka Field

Thesis, Spring 2008

The Zorrozaurre Zoological Garden of Cladistics:
Heterogeneous Surface Continuity through Digital Sculpting
Chris Shusta

Zoo Organization

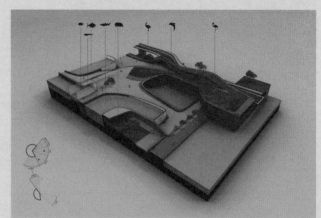

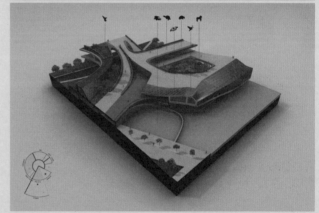

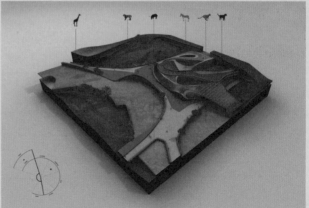

Different Zones of the Zoo

Non-Formal

Excerpt: Levittown Retrofitted:
An Urbanism Beyond the Property Line

Teddy Cruz
Lecture, March 4, 2008

It is very important to speculate viscerally about the conditions that surround us as practitioners. After September 11th, in my mind, a lot of the notions and speculations on different ideas of sovereignty and the dissolution of the political power of nation states began to become obsolete. When the debris of that unfortunate event began to clear, a very different world was revealed: a world once more divided by the clash of nations, by the imposition of the nation-state in demarcating formidable barriers across countries, separating jurisdictions and communities. This reinsertion of the global border, at an international level, has become a defining moment that invites us to critically analyze and reengage the conditions of crisis at the local level.

Playing in a very naïve way with these images, I began to speculate on what would occur if, by tracing an imaginary line across a world atlas, one were to extend the Tijuana-San Diego border, the place where I live and work. This speculative extension of the border would in fact form a trans-continental corridor between the 28th to

32nd north parallels. What emerged was something incredibly interesting. It coincided very much with the definition of the world's cartography by the Pentagon's new map, in which the world is once more divided, not any more between the third and the first worlds, but by what the Pentagon now calls the "non-integrated gap" 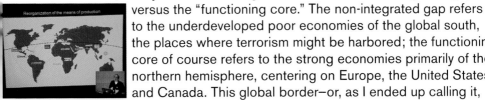 versus the "functioning core." The non-integrated gap refers to the underdeveloped poor economies of the global south, the places where terrorism might be harbored; the functioning core of course refers to the strong economies primarily of the northern hemisphere, centering on Europe, the United States, and Canada. This global border—or, as I ended up calling it, a political equator—is also where some of the most contested and dramatic social, economic, and political dynamics are at play as we speak, in the shape of hemispheric crossings. From the non-integrated gap, there is an unprecedented flow of migration as a Diaspora of Africans, Asians, and Latin Americans search for the strong economies of the functioning core, and settle primarily in Europe, the United States, and Canada. In the opposite direction, the politics of outsourcing and the redistribution of the means and centers of production begin to deploy the functioning core in search of the cheap labor markets of the non-integrated gap. The flow of migration is unprecedented: if this migrant nation were consolidated as a country, it would be the fourth largest country in the world. As this Diaspora settles in Europe, the United States, and Canada, it generates an illegal flow of capital that amounts to $200 billion annually; in Mexico alone, this amounts to more than $20 billion annually that immigrants from the United States send back to their countries and villages of origin. Of course, this amount of money is still completely off the radar of our institutions, and it's up for grabs in terms of how these informal economies or subsidies have an impact on the creation of infrastructure in many of these places.

Along this political equator, there is an amazing necklace of geographies of conflict, critical thresholds, and border zones. Beginning with the Tijuana-San Diego border, becoming the main funnel of migration from Latin America into the United States, and then to the Straight of Gibraltar—Ceuta and Melilla, which are becoming the main funnel of migration from North Africa into Europe—even picking up the Israeli-Palestinian border, and all the way to the other side of the world, to the dramatic transformations of the Chinese metropolis, equally out of urbanities of labor and surveillance. So this notion of a global conflict, of the reading of the geopolitics and economics at play, begins to redefine our ideas of the territory, and ultimately of practice. Conflict itself could be a way of redefining practice, as the exposure and the revealing of conflict at play can generate new critical correspondences between the global and the local.

The way in which this global conflict is reproduced at the local level, however, is missing a very important framework: the radicalization of the local in order to construct alternative readings of the global. In the last years we have been perpetrating the rhetoric of globalization at a very abstract level. The critical reading of these dynamics in the territory where I work and live, as these two cities recycle themselves and juxtapose and divide simultaneously, is very interesting: these flows across the border, these cross-border dynamics of people, goods, and services. This journey, from the notion of the global border down to the border neighborhood, is what has been of interest to my practice in the last seven years.

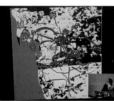

The Tijuana-San Diego checkpoint is the most trafficked border in the world. 60 million people cross it annually, not to mention the amazing amount of goods and services that percolate through this contested border. This socioeconomic funnel is once more compromised as Homeland Security is pouring billions of dollars to redefine the border ecology by inserting a huge project of infrastructure and surveillance, further barricading San Diego from Tijuana, and deploying an amazing matrix of paramilitary infrastructure. This mathematics of change in anticipation of the unknown now includes, a few miles away, a Fallujah in San Diego—mock Iraqi villages for training that even include the projected holograms of Arab subjects on the walls. This is a very sophisticated alliance between urbanization and militarization, unprecedented at the border: the intensification of a military section at the edge, now fused very conveniently with an anti-immigration policy. So these anti-terrorism, anti-immigration policies are again deploying an urbanism of fear ultimately packaged as a lifestyle in Southern California.

This perennial alliance of systems of control and development of urbanization and militarization is ultimately manifested physically in the border wall that transforms San Diego into the world's largest gated community. In the last thirty years the border territory in San Diego and Tijuana has hardened, and continues to harden, as Congress is ready to deploy hundreds of miles of new border walls. In tandem with the incremental hardening of the border wall, we have also noticed the hardening of social legislature and the erosion of public institutions and social programs toward the city as the urbanism of surveillance and fear is once more dividing communities, jurisdictions, and ultimately land uses.

Who would have imagined that the most compelling transborder urban tactics and strategies in the context of this top-down project of militarization would be in the hands of drug cartels, as they have dug some thirty tunnels between San Diego and Tijuana in the last eighty years, connecting garages to warehouses, churches to houses, on both sides of the border? The most compelling and dramatic of all is a two-way tunnel discovered recently. It was probably designed by an engineer; it had retaining walls, water extraction systems, electricity, ventilation, and it was two-way, so that while the drug cartel that commissioned the tunnel was not using it, they would lease it to coyotes crossing the border, making it, in fact, the first mixed-use tunnel across the border.

What I am suggesting is not the sensationalizing of these images, but the power of the informal densities and economies at play at the border that are still invisible to our institutions of representation, the kind of transactions and exchanges between these two cities that are completely off the radar of institutions. This condition of transgression— in fact, the border wall exists only to be transgressed—and the presence of the informal, in the shape of micro-urbanisms, have transformed my thinking.

The whole idea of how objects ultimately become operational systems is very interesting. Also the fact that what is imported and exported here are symbols of progress from one city to another. Who would have imagined that the urban code of Southern California, expressed by McMansions, would ultimately represent the desire of the whole world? You have all seen the dramatic images of Chinese developers building replicas of the gated communities of Southern California outside of Beijing, importing every cliché, including the cheap stock of fake tiles, stucco, and aluminum windows. But this is also what is happening at the edges of Tijuana, as the new liberalization of the banking industry and social housing subsidies has now brought private developers to build housing for the poor in Mexico. And this is what you find everywhere in Latin America: hundreds of little boxes in the shape of mini-masterplanned gated communities defining the edges of many of these cities, importing every cliché of their counterparts in the United States.

It's interesting that we have gone from one extreme to the other. As our profession contributed to the bastardization of the multifamily housing project after World War II, it became an ominous problem in terms of ghettoizing and creating social degradation;

now people are going to the other extreme and selling this project of privatized individual homes and individual lots as the new paradigm of social housing in many countries. But as people are sold this recipe of beige urbanism, they have now begun to retrofit it. I have been documenting how this recipe of homogeneity has begun to be pixelated as people try to inject socioeconomic contingencies into these dwellings. Isn't this ultimately the kind of utopian desire of architecture that comes back to us every thirty years or so? Can architecture transform out of socioeconomic contingency, and can architects or developers anticipate the mutation of these conditions?

As urban waste from San Diego flows southbound, recycled by Tijuana to build its own periphery, people go north in search of dollars, and the bulk of my research has been to understand the impact of immigration in the transformation of the American neighborhood. We notice again that for each of these mega-wealthy top-down projects of redevelopment everywhere in the world, there is another project that is produced: a project of marginalization. For each of these enclaves, there is a service sector or a service community that is needed to support them that we continue to ignore. Where are these sectors or rings of poverty located? What are these people doing? What is their role in the socioeconomic and cultural life of these environments?

There are two areas of interest in our profession at this moment, whether in academia, development, or governance. One is the redevelopment of downtowns everywhere out of the same recipes, from New York to San Diego: huge luxury condos surrounded by stadiums and the franchises that frame them. The same recipe of rampant privatization is everywhere, prompting a project of gentrification and displacement. On the other end, there is our interest in suburbia or at least sprawl, which is equally as wealthy.

The area that we continue to ignore—which for me has become the laboratory to really understand these dynamics further—is the area in between, which is in fact the first ring of suburbanization in many American cities. These older postwar neighborhoods are where many of these illegal 12 million illegal immigrants are settling, conveniently becoming the service sector for the expensive condos and hotels downtown and unable to afford rents in both extremes. We can speculate that some of these neighborhoods once looked like typical Levittowns, a homogeneous fabric of individual homes and individual lots. If we critically observe what has happened to this first ring of suburbanization in the last thirty or forty years, this homogeneity has begun to be pixelated by socioeconomic temporal dynamics, as immigrants have begun to retrofit many of these small bungalows, transforming them into other things. Our notions of density begin to transform in the context of these very interesting models.

I'm interested in the role of the informal, but within the American city—the pixelation of these environments with difference, with socioeconomic temporalities, with the informal—to understand what it can do to produce very different ideas of policy. If that has happened—and it's unavoidable and clear it has happened to the first ring of sub-urbanization in the last thirty or forty years—and if our institutions continue to ignore or be unable to measure the dynamics of this transformation, can we speculate that in the next sixty to a hundred years, the third, fourth, fifth, or sixth rings of suburbaniza-tion will go through the same destiny, and that the McMansions that are now being built on the edges of San Diego, with 9,000 square feet for one family, will have to be retrofitted for difference, in particular as conditions of environmental crisis become more pressing?

It seems to me that, as we engage this urbanization of retrofitting and of adaptation, the pixelation of the large with the small will define the terms of Southern California's future. Of course, this is the kind of debate that has been present in academia and beyond in the last ten years: what to do with our obsession with style, where every single guide-line in every masterplanned community defines what style we should build in, while ignoring the socioeconomic and political processes that are truly redefining the city.

By straddling the border between the politics of discriminatory zoning in San Diego and the tactics of the informal in Tijuana, my practice inserts itself in the middle of these dynamics. The condition is very clear. At least for my practice, it has been important to reveal a phenomenon, to expose a crisis and the conflicts behind it. The dismantling of those conflicts is the key to producing a very different process of intervention and recuperating a political voice for our profession.

Dirty Work: Transforming Landscape in the Non-Formal City of the Americas

Christian Werthmann, John Beardsley, curators
Exhibition, January 28–March 14, 2008

The exhibition presented new terrain and tactics for landscape architecture. One subject was physical: low-income communities, variously called squatter settlements, shantytowns, or slums, which are a dominant feature of megacities in the developing world. The other was professional: the new activist and entrepreneurial practices that attempt to operate in these circumstances, among the most challenging imaginable.

The exhibition presented the various ways that contemporary designers are attempting to upgrade these settlements physically without destroying them socially, saving what they can of their physical structure while alleviating environmental and social problems ranging from inadequate public space and housing to unemployment, insecure land tenure, and unsanitary conditions. The exhibition focused on Latin America, using landscape as the particular lens through which to examine these settlements: their occupation of marginal lands in floodplains or on steep slopes; their separation from urban landscape infrastructure, be it roads, transportation, sewers, water supply, or storm-water management; their severe environmental, public health, and security problems; and their lack of public facilities for economic, cultural, or recreational activities. Landscape is conceptualized as both the primary problem and the main opportunity for these communities.

What is "dirty" about this work? It addresses itself to massive economic, environmental, infrastructural, and social failures of recent urban policies, and it often involves the messy procedures of community design and the compromises of political action. At the same time, it is arguably complicit in neoliberal policies that favor microenterprise and market-based solutions over more ambitious, state-sponsored initiatives that might have a larger impact. It is not yet clear if upgrading can achieve significant permanent improvements or if it will merely perpetuate social and spatial inequalities,
with large percentages of the population packed into disproportionately small
areas and cut off from basic services. In the current economic and political climate,
however, such "Dirty Work" might be a designer's most viable mode of practice in
the context of the non-formal city.

Apart from climate change, there are few greater challenges to widespread planetary health and security than the proliferation of non-formal settlements. As difficult and complex as conditions are in these communities, however, they provide clues to their own improvement: residents of non-formal cities often display cultural adaptations and survival strategies that can guide future interventions. It is becoming the role of designers to give spatial form to the environmental, social, and economic ambitions of these communities, helping to marshal the financial investment and political will to begin their transformation. The exhibition explored the relationship between social ethics and creativity in design culture, advancing the hopeful thesis that impoverished contexts do not have to result in a poverty of imagination.

Cities featured in the exhibition were: Bogotá, Colombia; Buenos Aires, Argentina; Caracas, Venezuela; Mexico City and Tijuana, Mexico; and Rio de Janeiro and São Paulo, Brazil.

Scale and Distribution of Informal Settlements

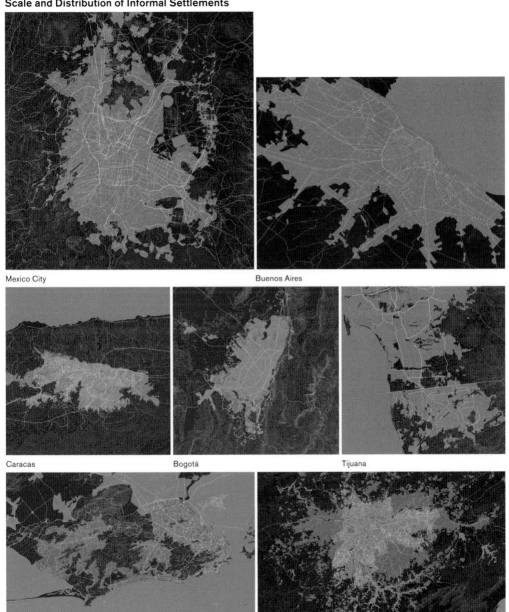

Mexico City

Buenos Aires

Caracas

Bogotá

Tijuana

Rio de Janeiro

São Paulo

Non-Formal Settlements
- World Population 2000
- Slum Population 2000
- World Population Growth 2020
- Slum Population Growth 2020
- Population Loss 2020
- Fewer Slums 2020

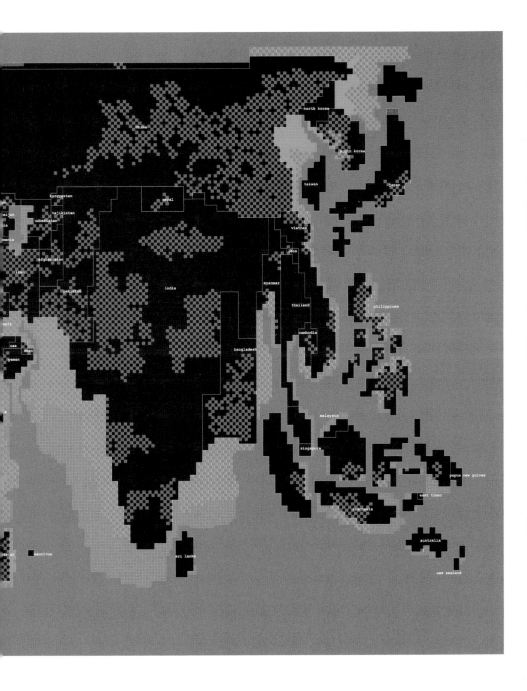

Economics of Informality and Modes of Practice

Reclaiming Utopia:
Reality and Initiative in the City of Nairobi

Chi-Yan Chan, Emily Farnham, Sondra Fein, Benny Ho, Meehae Kwon, Yusun Kwon;
Jacques Herzog, Pierre de Meuron, advisors
Independent Thesis, Fall 2007–Spring 2008 Teaching Associate: Manuel Herz. Support: Elise Jaffe, Jeffrey Brown. Assistance: Ligia Nobre; Shadi Rahbaran; ETH Studio Basel Group, Fall 2007; The University of Nairobi. Nairobi Workshop Basel Participants: Davinder Lamba, Alfred Omenya, Paul Syagga, Evalyne Wanyama.

After Metrobasel, the Canary Islands, Naples, Paris, and the publication of studies on Switzerland as a thoroughly urbanized country, this series of international urban portraits continues with the study of Nairobi. In previous years, GSD in collaboration with Studio Basel has developed a set of tools and identified themes and agendas that are central to its study of cities in transformation. Instead of understanding the city as a system composed of binary opposites, such as formal and informal areas, the study attempts to unfold the complex simultaneity and dependencies of these parameters by carefully tracing the basic human activities within the spaces in which they unfold. Instead of an approach centered around these perceived grand dichotomies, the study focuses on activities at the local scale. Research methods developed previously, such as precise observation and mapping tools, obtain an urgency and a pivotal (political) significance in an environment where facts are often opaque and space is the medium where debates, negotiations of power, and conflict are played out.

Can we think of Nairobi as an ordinary city? Can we study Nairobi in terms of its basic human activities? Can we investigate how the city functions by looking at how people live and work, or how people move through the city? Can we challenge the predominant approach to "the African City" that focuses mostly on issues of development, disparate temporalities, and binary opposites like formal and informal? This approach, witnessed in recent examples of urban portraits of the African continent, fails to register complexities on the ground, falling back to a mere repetition of clichés and coming dangerously close to replicating a (post-)colonialist standpoint.

The notion of reclaiming one's territory and of taking back both the physical and the ideological ground that was lost through colonization (and not fully regained in the early post-independence governments) is at the heart of Nairobi's positive dynamic entrepreneurial spirit, and also what plagues the city and nation in its struggle for equitable and fair governance and economy. The post-election events of late 2007 and early 2008 underscore the urgency of this study, and reveal the complexity and the challenges of the present circumstances in Kenya's capital city. With a careful tracing of Nairobi's history and a thorough study of specific facets of its daily life, it may be possible to draw the city—metaphorically and physically—with both specificity and broadness. Beyond thorough description and informed speculation, the goal is to give this portrait back to Nairobians, in the hope that it will be revealing to those who live in the city but may never have seen themselves in this way before.

Excerpt: Let's Go Shopping!
Chi-Yan Chan

Excerpt: Work It Nairobi
Emily Farnham

Excerpt: Re-Creating Nairobi
Sondra Fein

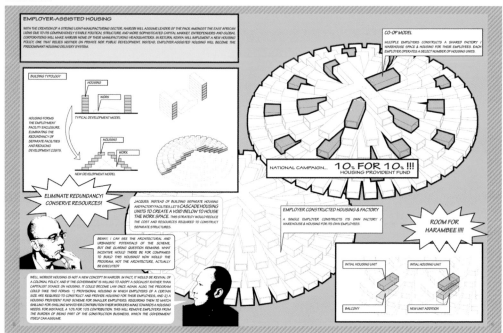

Excerpt: Living It Up
Benny Ho

Excerpt: Learner's Paradise
Meehae Kwon

Excerpt: Keep It Moving
Yusun Kwon

Excerpt: NOW?

Abdou Maliq Simone
Dialogue, April 24, 2008

As an opening proviso, I want to talk about what some of us are thinking about in terms of what is called black urbanism. Black urbanism refers to the ways in which the multiplicity of experiences of black urban residents in different parts of the world might constitute an archive in helping us think about urban politics in many different kinds of cities: not just those of Africa, but also beyond. It refers to an urban politics which seems to be increasingly characterized by the loss of efficacy, of forms of political mobilization which tended to rely upon a whites-based advocacy of the inclusion of the excluded, of forms of local governance which were able to more adequately represent the needs of particular kinds of residents, particularly those of the so-called urban poor to maintain viable places of operation within municipal systems. It is a politics that, instead of an emphasis on mutual accommodation, reciprocity, consensus-building, partnerships—the kinds of descriptions that characterize what constitutes an effective politics within municipal systems—seems to be counterbalanced by the realities of an intersection amongst heterogeneities, one that is often conflictual and problematic, where different kinds of actors and ways of life take each other into consideration, but use that consideration to amplify their own particularities and autonomies, in an almost fractal positionality in relation to the city as a whole. This kind of politics is not easily characterized by the conventional tropes of effective local urban governance that has been in some sense the consensus of most policy-makers over the past twenty-five years.

Black urban residents have historically had to maneuver their life in cities in terms of lines of inclusion and exclusion, where those lines are always shifting in terms of the kinds of historical junctures, policies, and self-organizations that have enabled specific black populations in particular places to construct a sense of being either included or excluded. This kind of "doubleness" is perhaps a platform or archive which allows us to have ideas about a doubled intensification for many urban residents everywhere: an entanglement of possibility and precarity. In thinking about urban futures in many cities, particularly large cities across the urban South, there seems to be the sense that urban life is becoming more possible, in terms of the diminution and wearing away of particular kinds of mediations, institutions, and discourses that tended to anchor urban populations within particular territories, sectors, or ways of calculating what their possibilities are, and in the broader opening up of the different networks that urban residents are participating in: the kinds of jobs they actually do, the very practices which put bread on the table. But that very source of possibility also makes people vulnerable, because the diminution of those very mediations and mechanisms of translation and social anchorage in particular urban territories also makes people much more precarious. It is this entanglement of precarity and possibility which perhaps the experiences of black urban residents at different historical junctures, having to negotiate this doubleness of inclusion and exclusion, might enable us to know something about.

Here there is no reference to any culturally authentic source of origins but the ability to look upon a wide canvass of struggles undertaken by peoples of African ancestry and put them together as an invented universe of operation in which the practice of self-organization in the present can contextualize as "its world".

Part of the problematic in which the use of blackness as a device is situated is the sense, which we know well from contemporary urban life, of the possibilities in which all different kinds of things and actors within the city can be brought together in close proximity without really having to pay attention or to deal with each other. And so notions of regulation, governance, discipline, and control within cities have a diminished reliance upon territorial markers or the separation of populations as a way to maintain control, to regulate the way in which diversities and heterogeneities engage each other, intersect with each other, or productively do something unantici-pated with each other. Though there has been a lot of emphasis on the reintensifica-tion of spatial segregation and polarization, we know increasingly the kinds of proficiencies through which very diverse aspects of urban life can assume a kind of territorial proximity without really having to take each other into consideration, with only limited substantive interpenetration.

As the field of our attention becomes more expansive, the capacities for dismissal become more extensive and arbitrary. The more we have to pay attention to differ-ent kinds of things, the more the decision of what we pay attention to becomes more arbitrary, because there is no effective map that says how you do it; the more arbitrary they become, the more we tend to exclude things for reasons that we cannot account to ourselves. In this field of intensified arbitrariness, what we are really doing is reproducing the kind of field that race opened up in the first place. Race first had its traction as a way to make arbitrary decisions. Who gets to be taken seriously and who doesn't? Who gets to live and who doesn't? Who has recourse to making certain kinds of appeal based on their capacity, based upon what they know, based upon their skills? Race becomes the arbiter of what gets dismissed and what doesn't. Somehow, then, the arbitrary essence of racial distinction remains a key historical underpinning of this intensification of a field of arbitrariness—even though race may not be mentioned, even though blackness and whiteness may no longer be the criteria through which those kinds of arbitrary decisions are made.

Given this kind of extension, then, black urbanism refers to a kind of responsibility that the city is something to be made not just in terms of calculations of equanim-ity, justice, or fairness, but that the city is still something to be made without maps: something beyond surveillance, beyond risk analysis. Blackness is a commitment to make something without clear certainties in the face of dispersals of control and the increasingly ephemeral compositions of regulatory power that once had a much more visible face. The commitment to do the kind of work that is necessary for many districts to do in order to maintain their economic and political viability, to keep themselves from being simply wiped away or effaced, has a lot to do with a certain willingness to operate and act without such clear maps; the notion of blackness is in some sense a metaphor for this kind of responsibility, as the inverse of the intensifi-cation of arbitrariness which redivides the city in terms of a multiplicity of exclusions and inclusions which don't necessarily have territorial parameters.

These kinds of skills require a wide range of reciprocities, transactions and collaboration. What haunts the modern urban experience may be precisely these more invisible modalities of sociality that circumvent normative mechanisms of social exchange; as such, black urbanism accounts for the more shadow-like dimensions of urban life. Seemingly outside the ordering processes, capacities and networks of late modernity, these contemporary shadows accommodate what Nigel Thrift has talked about as fugitive materials: bits and pieces of traditions, codes, jettisoned and patchworked economies, pirated technologies, bits and pieces and symbols that increasingly find their way into all cities, that accompany practices of evasion, trespassing, circumvention, and dissimulation, that reflect the determination of those without secure urban positions to maintain the viability of life.

When one goes into any of the major markets of Abidjan, Lagos, or Dwala, one sees that there are two to three times as many people in these markets daily who are not selling or buying anything. They're in the market because the market is part of their job; and their job is, in some sense working, with all of these fugitive materials. The market is a circulation of rumor, of gossip, of prices; of different kinds of information; of different words, of glances, of affect; of people coming with different kinds of anxieties, different kinds of hopes, different kinds of expectations. The majority of people who operate in the market on a daily basis are those that try to put these kinds of things together, even to the extent where many markets now become in some ways the bundling of these different kinds of commodities. So people are no longer selling a bag of rice, or a case of beer, or some electric cable; they're selling a bundle of electric cable with rice, with beer, with a promise to fix your water pump for six months, with a promise that you will get an introduction when the Minister of Education's son comes to visit his aunt in the neighborhood next week, so that hopefully your high school kid will now be able to go to a good school with a reduced price... This whole package is sold for a particular kind of price. What is this price, which doesn't operate in terms of conventional economics, and how is it worked out? It is worked out and changes almost daily, in terms of what people are talking about, imagining, thinking is possible. These more invisible socialities are not just a kind of ephemera that exists in the background, but are brought into the very center of the marketplace, as the space which concretizes the contemporary urban economy.

This, then, is the important political position which many, particularly African, urban residents assume: a kind of doubleness. Because if you've tried to do all the right things—if you've tried to save money to send your kids to school; if you've gone to university; if you hope that working for that degree will give you a job in the civil service, which doesn't pay much, but would let you buy a small house, and with which you can send your children to a decent school and put food on the table—and yet you find out that you have to wait twelve years after your university degree in order to get your first formal job; if you discover that you have to skip meals, that you can have lunch every other day and dinner every other day; if you find that you've saved enough money to send your child to school—but no teachers show up; if you find that you've done all

Nairobi, 2008

the right things and it doesn't pay off, then how do you survive? Through these kinds of shadow economies, the piecing together of all these fugitive materials which have constituted the real economy through which the majority of urban residents, particularly in Africa, have been able to maintain a viable position in the city. But that kind of trajectory will never have enough money, never be resourced enough, never have the kind of political support or the time to truly institutionalize itself as a real alternative. It doesn't have a sufficient institutional base that people can count on it as a kind of future. But neither does doing the "right thing" in terms of all the modern practices of urban life. So people are in some sense caught between a rock and a hard place: if you go with either one, you don't have a viable future. So you have to negotiate an affiliation with both. You have to continue to commit yourself both to a kind of modern practice which you know isn't going to get you anywhere, and with a shadowed urban existence which reproduces a kind of viability but doesn't take you anywhere beyond that. You double your chances within this kind of affiliation.

What this produces in terms of the daily experience of everyday life is an intense generosity, but also inexplicable violence, because one cannot have a rational anchorage on which to hang both of these hats in trying to negotiate this kind of doubleness. It is this kind of effort, this kind of day-to-day political positionality, which the conventional discourses of political mobilization and urban development, as purported by NGOs and by the policy-making apparatus, simply cannot come to grips with.

The relationship between formality and informality is often a product of how one pays attention. For example, within many African large cities under colonial regimes, African residents had no rights; they had no formal status. They were provisional labor; they had the right to work within the city for a certain length of time and to operate in certain spaces, but very little opportunity to institutionalize any product of those efforts. On the other hand, as long as white people were satisfied that Africans weren't really doing anything that challenged their control over the city as a whole, they didn't really pay that much attention. They let Africans do their thing in the spaces to which they were consigned. That's a particular product of a way of visibility and a way of paying attention. If one had looked, if one had tried to pay attention to what was happening in those spaces, there would be activities which we would recognize as somewhat informal and provisional. But there were efforts to regularize things, to induce and compel certain kinds of stabilities, to write contracts, to make things that lasted, to have things like memberships, to have written orders of things. They had no formal status within the prevailing rules of formality of the municipal system itself, but to say that they were informal would not be giving them their due. So, in some ways, what is formal or informal is the product of a certain visualization; it's a particular way of paying attention. When something works, people try to stabilize it, to make it consistent over time; it may look informal in terms of its composition, but in terms of its status in people's lives, it becomes an anchor, a kind of stability.

Here the collaboration with architects could be very important. The tendency is to rush in and make something nice and neat; people want things that look nice; they want good living conditions and things that work. The mistake of policymakers is often to come in and say they're going to take care of everything, rather than seeing that the problem itself provides an opportunity for people to collaborate in ways that they otherwise might not. How do architects interface with that kind of logic? How do they extend their skills to resist the temptation to solve the problem once and for all, but to do something more provisional? Something of those kinds of negotiations, I think, are important.

Core III Architecture, Fall 2007

Boston Greenway, YMCA

1 Andrew Lantz   **2** Yair Keshet

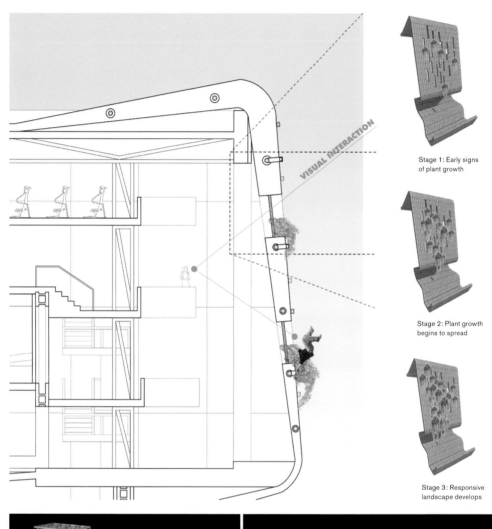

VISUAL INTERACTION

Stage 1: Early signs of plant growth

Stage 2: Plant growth begins to spread

Stage 3: Responsive landscape develops

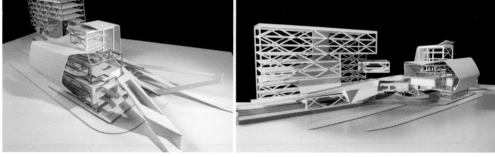

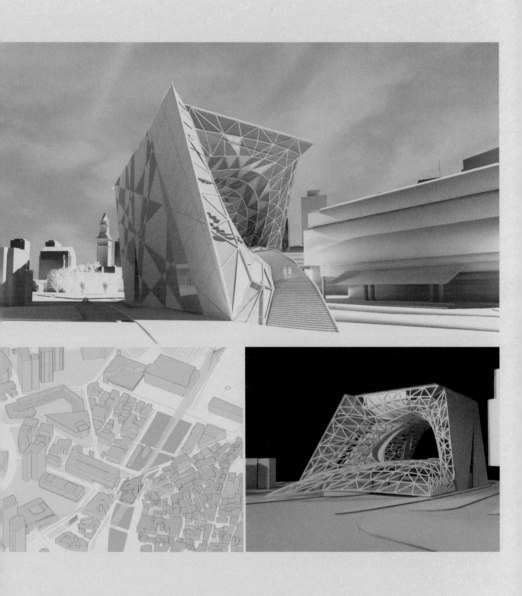

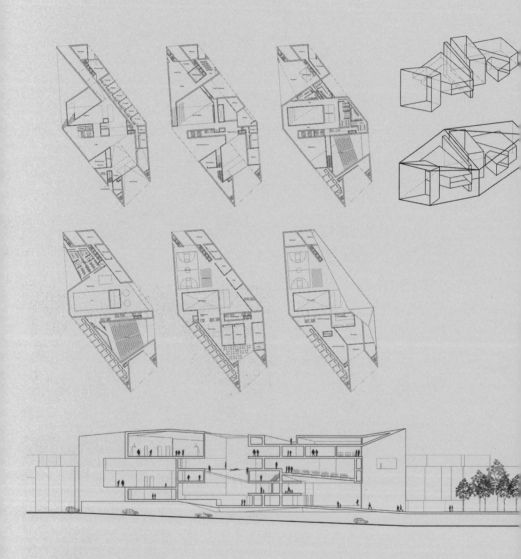

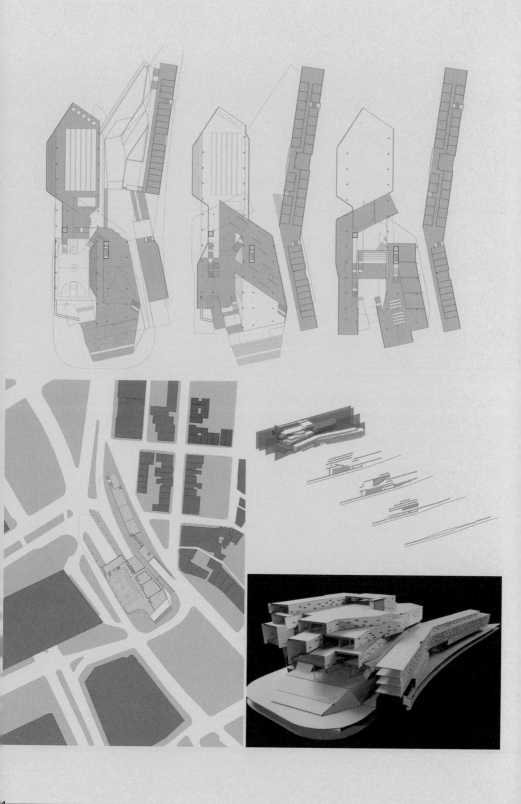

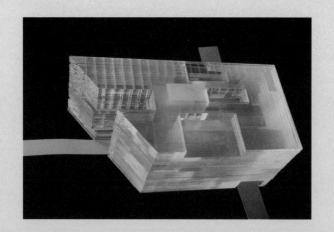

Level 1

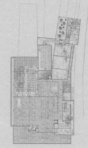

Level 2

Level 3

Level 4

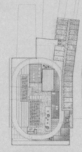

Level 5

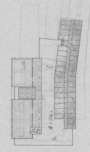

Level 6

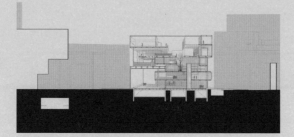

Four key views in the form of commemorative plates

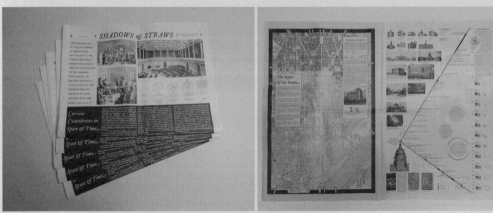

Research document in the form of broadsheet newspaper

Thesis, Spring 2008

Metrocosm: City in the Sprawl | Stage One: The Catalytic Metamorphosis of the Shopping Mall
Duy Ho

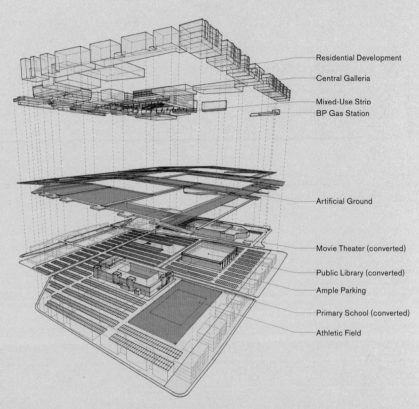

Residential Development
Central Galleria
Mixed-Use Strip
BP Gas Station

Artificial Ground

Movie Theater (converted)
Public Library (converted)
Ample Parking
Primary School (converted)
Athletic Field

Exploded layers of the project

Night view

New street

Typology

Verticalism (The Future of the Skyscraper)

Iñaki Abalos
Essay, 2008

Modern architects associated the skyscraper with the organization of work, of offices. In fact, the prototypical skyscraper of modernity is the very expression of this same organization: the optimal means to sort and connect workers who sort and connect data. This reification of bureaucracy—outside of any pejorative connotation—was interpreted symbolically by those best equipped, like Mies van der Rohe, in terms of rectilinear prisms of steel and glass, artificially climatized, organized in rings around nuclei of vertical communication. Buildings like the Seagram in New York, and in Spain the fabulous BBV by Sáenz de Oiza, gave definitive form to this conception. But they forgot (or it was not yet the right moment for) the multiple possibilities opened by vertical construction, and which we have seen multiplying over the last decades along with the global growth of the economy and the demographic expansion of Southeast Asia. The immense majority of skyscrapers built today are located in Asia, they are residential, their structure is concrete, and they are naturally ventilated, lacking any monumental aura: they are products of consumption. Without exaggeration it could be said that all contemporary metropolises are leading toward densification, which even the most recalcitrant mayors have begun to understand as an instrument with which they should become familiar. Meanwhile, many European and American architects who until a few years ago monopolized the typology appear to have been overtaken by its iconic character, and the discourse of the skyscraper has closed itself into a self-referential verticality, or at best a representation of capital and its excesses, as if we were witnessing a terminal, mannerist phase of the history of the typology.

The skyscrapers developed in Madrid, for example—with the notable exception of the brilliant exercise realized by the office of Rubio and Alvarez-Sala—have fallen once more into the hands of foreign architects of that generation which, though they dazzled occasionally in the 1970s, have spent two decades boring us at the global scale; that is, boring the critics and citizens of the world. The weak popular and professional echo of the built results—with their lazy repertoire of a mediocre city, with no capacity to move us, in contrast to the visibility of the new scale they introduce—shows that something has gone wrong.

But the coming reality is decidedly different. Nothing could be farther away from the vulgar case of Madrid than the future of the skyscraper. In reality, "verticalism," the conception of the space of the contemporary city in vertical terms, has only begun. We are witnessing an exciting process of transformation. We have begun to think of the city—and of historic cities—from positions which effectively substitute the bidimensionality of urbanism for a new verticalism. It remains to be seen if this position refers to a complementary form of, or an alternative to, thinking about the city: in plan or in 3D, urbanism or verticalism. In the professional work of the generation of forty and fifty year-olds, and of the youngest architects, we are seeing the flourishing of vertical libraries, vertical laboratories, vertical fashion buildings, vertical university campuses, vertical museums, vertical parks, vertical sports centers—such that combinations of all these, mixed with residential typologies, hotels, and offices, conjoin at times to produce real cities, in which the building section becomes what the urban plan has represented up to now (mixed-use buildings). On the other hand, mixing towers with distinct uses but with a single formal logic, creating a group or cluster of towers, is an effective and opportune alternative for large vertical mixed-use programs in many contexts (the so-called bundle of towers). They have the virtue of displacing interest to objects in the air that surround one another, to the space they create, and to the form in which these new constructions interact with existing ones. They transfer the once-iconic charge of the autobiographical object into public space, into the city they generate.

Politicians and architects should attend to this new flowering of skyscrapers since they add new qualities and enormous capacities and degrees of freedom to maneuver if they are used toward public ends, giving place to forms of beauty whose exploration will surely be one of the central themes of architects and architectural schools in the years to come. Historical cities can also find many solutions through strategies of infiltration by smaller towers, strategies of "acupuncture" which, faced with the boulevard of Hausmannian Paris, have the benefit of the minimum footprint with the maximum capacity for transformation. While other cities like Rotterdam, Paris, or Turin propose to serially increment the density of their centers through this strategy (taking advantage of neutral holes with the least affection from their neighbors), Spanish cities, in spite of numerous proposals that have been recognized in different competitions, still brood over the benefits of using their open spaces and infrastructures serially, constructively, to benefit the city—to use their open potentials for a renewed conception of verticality, a universal phenomenon that modifies routines and opens a space of optimism and difference. The successful experience of modern skyscrapers centered essentially in private business should be reverted and rethought for public benefit or for the agreement of both, essaying new modalities of urban organization that prefigure the future. The incorporation of this revision of institutional and public typologies, which have for a century been anchored to 19th-century organizations, has also begun to signal a certain adaptation in the institutional terrain.

The public spaces made possible by this more strategic contemporary verticalism, with its small mark on sites and the obvious sustainability it provides in using the distinct activities of its section synergetically, are factors that have an ever-greater weight in its acceptance. The public space generated historically by skyscrapers—that mix of commercial streets and picturesque parks inaugurated by the invention of Central Park in New York, with its capacity to transform Midtown—surely contains the genetic code for contemporary public space. Trees and skyscrapers feed each other naturally, making their amalgam one of the true leitmotifs of contemporary architecture.

Verticalism is a strategy that can permit historic cities to continue exercising their weight in a future of extreme competition that is already here.

Super Tall studio final review, Fall 2007

Urban Sports Culture:
A New Stadium for Club Atlético Boca Juniors

Jorge Silvetti

Options Studio, Spring 2008 **Students:** Elizabeth Christoforetti, Nathan Fash, Sylvia Feng, Meredith Kole, Min Ter Lim, Sheng-Wei Lo, Noel Moreno, Saverio Panata, Pedro Santa Rivera, Leah Solk, Gregory Spaw, Saif Vagh, Kent Wu, Soo Jin Yoo. **Teaching Assistant:** Pedro Santa Rivera. **Participants:** Alberto (Tito) Varas, Daniel Becker, Nicolas Bares, Juan Frigerio, Federico Garcia Zuñiga, Marcelo Lorelli (Buenos Aires), Lluis Ortega, Hanif Kara.

This studio addressed the issues and challenges involved in the design of a world-class soccer stadium in the neighborhood of La Boca in Buenos Aires, a soccer-loving city with a long and rich tradition of urban stadia. In addition to the typical technical and functional demands that such structures pose to the designer, in this case it was required to weave into the stadium fabric the complex and subtle cultural and urbanistic conditions that define a unique context, in order to produce an artifact of extraordinary physical and symbolic presence in the city. Students first researched the history of stadia from classical times to the present, including an analysis of paradigmatic buildings that set standards from antiquity (e.g., the Roman Coliseum) to the most advanced recent examples (e.g., Herzog and de Meuron's "bird's nest" in Beijing). This phase was followed by an analysis of the particular characteristics of two selected and very diverse alternative sites in the neighborhood of La Boca: one tightly embedded within the urban fabric itself (as has been traditional in Buenos Aires) and adjacent to the old Stadium, the second across a water canal that would place it facing the La Boca neighborhood, thus presenting itself as a city icon on the waterfront. This included a study of the area's history as a distinctive socio-ethno-cultural district in an urban conglomerate of over thirteen million people, its identification with the internationally famed Boca Juniors soccer team, and the impact that current major infrastructural projects would have in its development. Of particular attention were the issues raised by the insertion of this large and peculiar structure within La Boca's fabric of low building density and high population density.

After these initial phases of research, study, and design hypothesis-building, students traveled to Buenos Aires for a week-long field trip where they experienced Buenos Aires' "urban sports culture" in action first-hand, received instruction from local experts, presented their in-progress proposals to a group of local academics and professionals, and made their own surveys and observations. Back at Harvard, projects were reviewed from a structural engineering perspective in a special session, and the final projects were reviewed by instructors from other schools in the United States and South America, and from within the GSD.

Existing Club Atlético Boca Juniors stadium, 2008

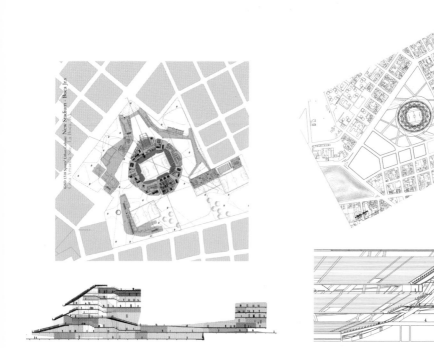

Pedro Santa Rivera ———————————————————— **Kent Wu** ——

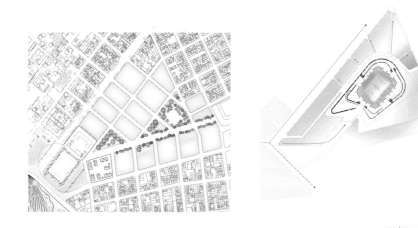

Nathan Fash ————————————————————— **Sheng Wei-Lo** ——

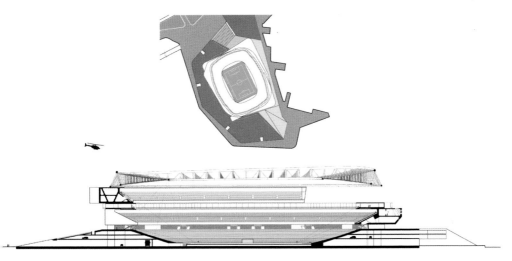

Saverio Panata

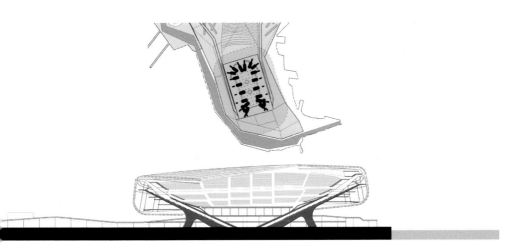

Min Ter Lim

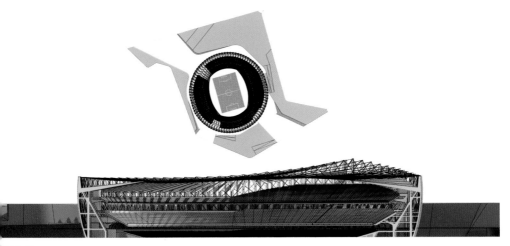

Sylvia Feng

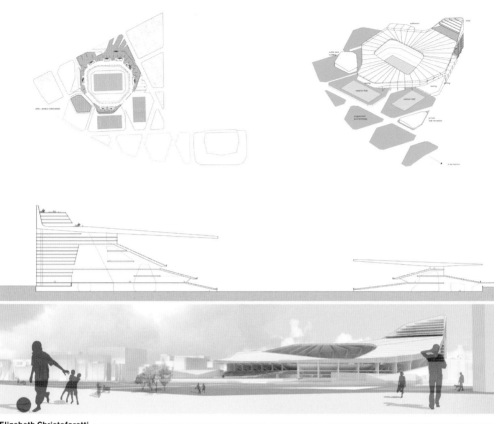

Elizabeth Christoforetti

Skin

Bowl

Hung
Floorplates

Pitch

Ticketing
Lobby

Structure/
Vertical
Circulation

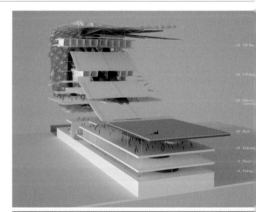
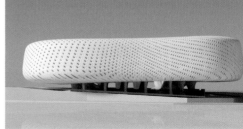

Min Ter Lim

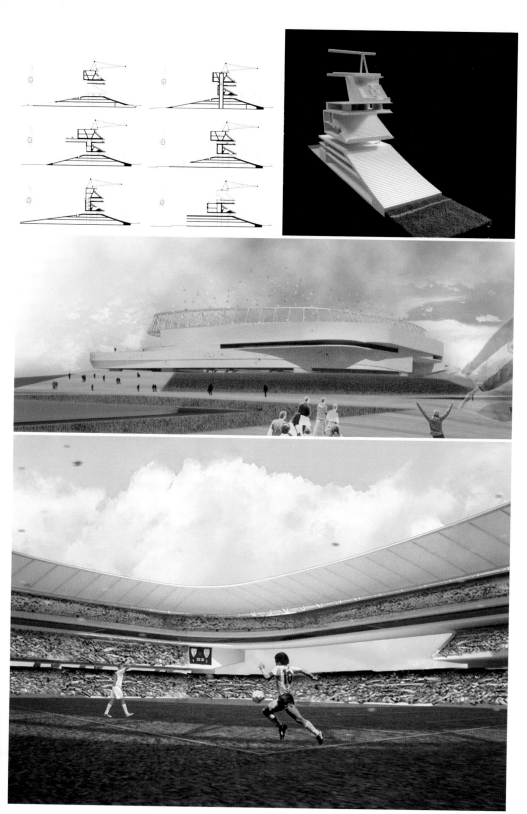

Saverio Panata

Slanted Memorial: Housing For Separated Families at the DMZ, Korea

Jin Young Song
Thesis, Fall 2007

The issue of separated families in Korea is a tragic and distorted one. The story begins with the Korean War, from 1950 to 1953. During these three years, roughly one million civilians were killed or wounded, and another 1.2 million lost their family members and homes. After this intense conflict, both sides agreed to establish a buffer zone dividing the two sides, the Demilitarized Zone, which exists today. At 155 miles long and approximately 2.5 miles wide, the Demilitarized Zone is the most heavily armed border in the world. Except for the Joint Security Area and occasional small clashes, there has been absolutely no passing for half a century. On opposite sides of this border, both sides have tried to construct their own memory about the past. Officially, the war is not over.

Since 2000 there have been roughly ten meeting events for separated families between the two sides, through the "sunshine policy" of the South Korean government. Once a year, at Seoul and Pyongyang, 100 families are exchanged for a 2–3 night hotel stay; afterwards, they return to their sides with no promise to meet again. These "fortunate" cases represent just 2.5% of all applicants for these meetings.

What is needed is housing on a new site which is in neither the North nor the South, outside the land of any country.

The thesis proposes a memorial and housing. While usually a memorial is built after an event to commemorate it, I propose a memorial to commemorate ongoing events—the lives of the separated families. They are the only remaining sacred artifacts in this history, and a form of memory both sides can share and mourn together. The memorial creates witnesses to our past and present.

The project symbolizes this situation as a form of memorial through the use of the slant. The tilt of the housing box symbolizes the ideological dispute and tragic history between North and South Korea. Architecturally, it transforms the bottom face of the housing into a main façade of the memorial.

View of housing within DMZ

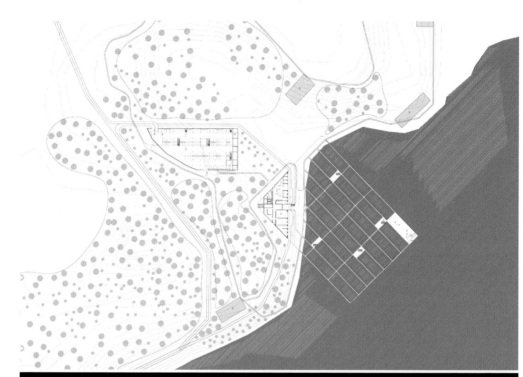

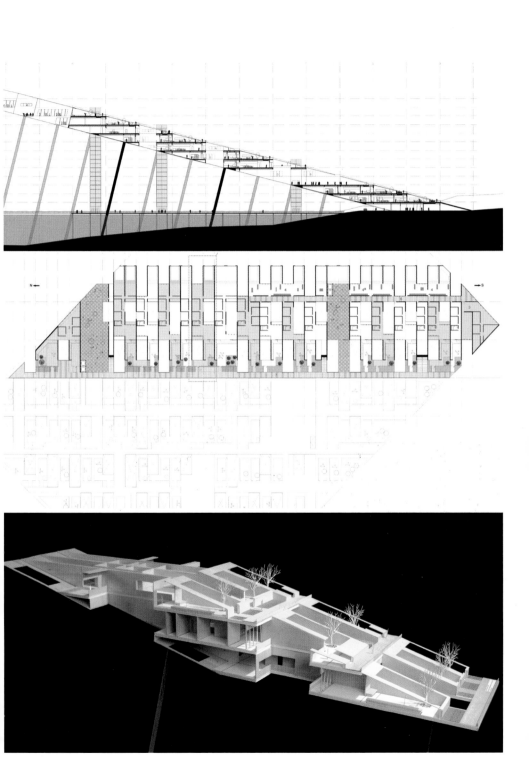

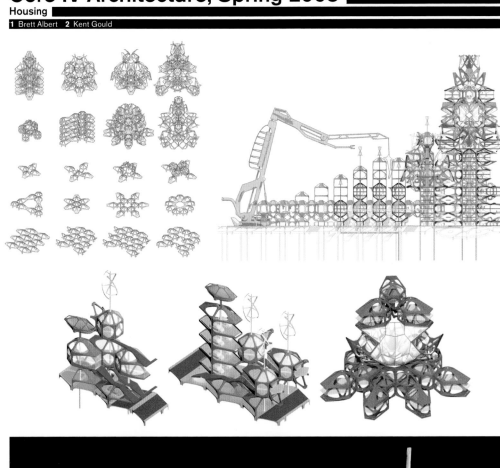

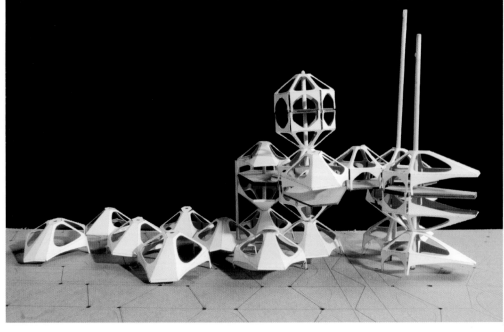

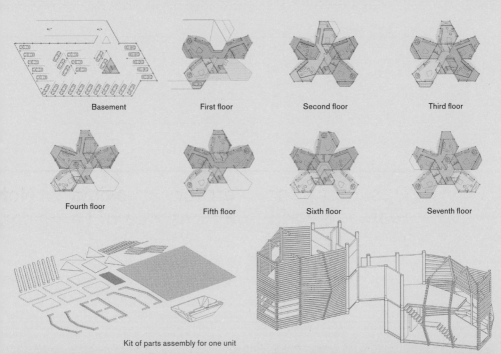

Basement   First floor   Second floor   Third floor

Fourth floor   Fifth floor   Sixth floor   Seventh floor

Kit of parts assembly for one unit

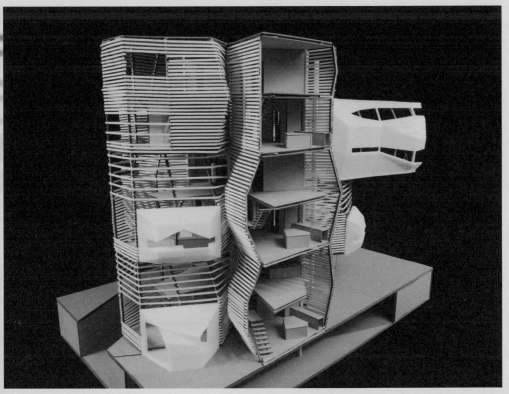

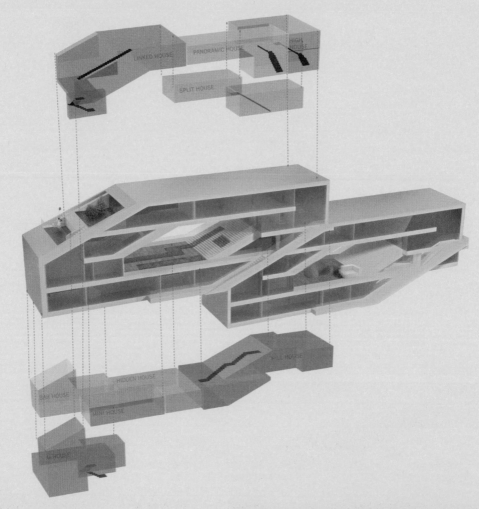

LINKED HOUSE PANORAMIC HOUSE HIGH HOUSE

SPLIT HOUSE

HILL HOUSE

HIDDEN HOUSE

BAR HOUSE

MINI HOUSE

U HOUSE

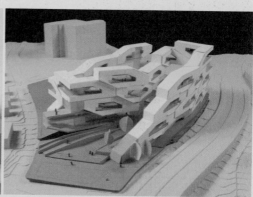

Core IV Architecture, Spring 2008

Housing

5 Johannes Kohnle   **6** Matthew Allen

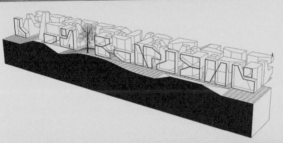

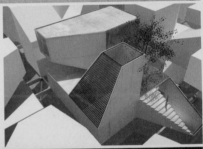

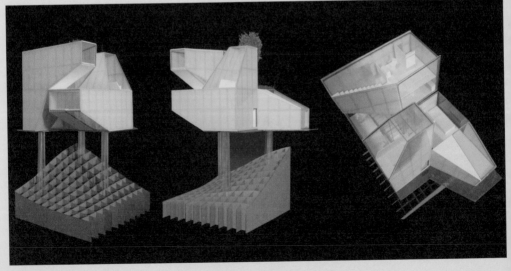

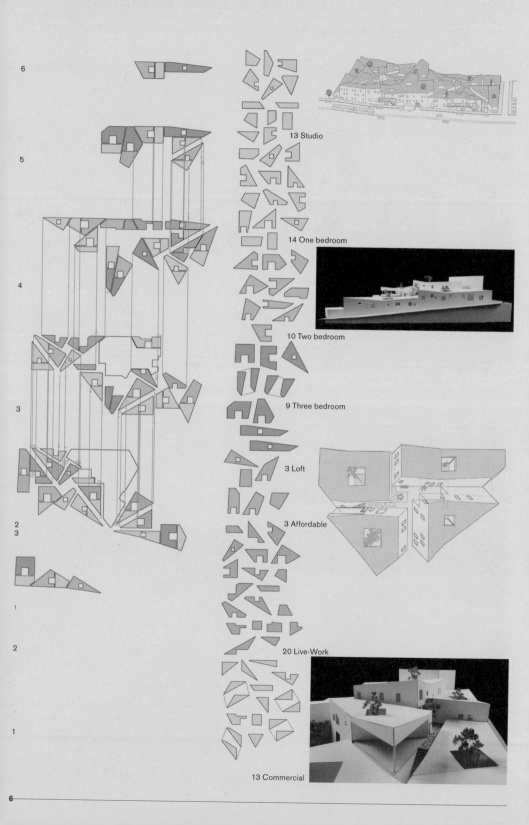

13 Studio

14 One bedroom

10 Two bedroom

9 Three bedroom

3 Loft

3 Affordable

20 Live-Work

13 Commercial

6

5

4

3

2
3

1

2

1

Thesis, Spring 2008

[Re] Activating the Senses within a Blurred Contemporary Reality: Site Specific Apertures
Justin Szeremeta

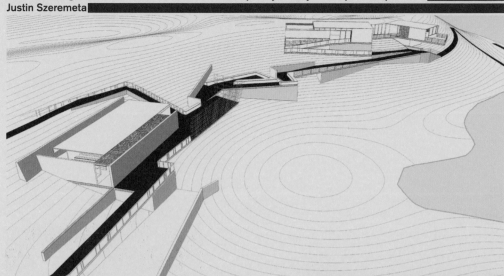

Ramp leading to forum space

View of exterior dining

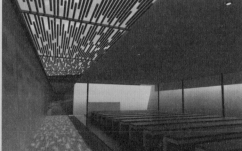

Interior lighting in the assembly space

Thesis, Fall 2008

Production and Performance: An Approach to Discarded Landsites on Industrial Waterfronts

Jonathan Rule

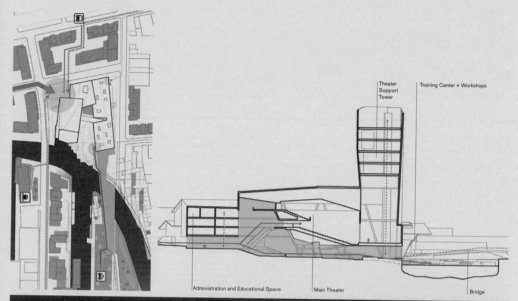

Theater Support Tower

Training Center + Workshops

Administration and Educational Space

Main Theater

Bridge

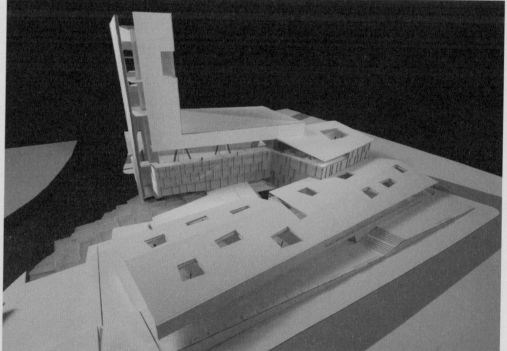

Geographies

Design, Agency, Territory—Provisional Notes on Planning and the Emergence of Landscape

Charles Waldheim
Excerpted from *New Geographies* (Harvard GSD), Issue 0, April 2008

This first issue of *New Geographies* inaugurates an ambitious yet timely editorial mandate. One of the aims of the journal is to examine recent claims made by the design disciplines on the larger territorial subjects traditionally associated with geography and planning. This and future editions of the journal seek to describe the "expanded agency" of the designer as the design disciplines reengage with the larger forces and flows of economy and ecology. This mandate acknowledges the fluidity of disciplinary identities that have been characteristic of the design fields over the past decade. It equally suggests an ongoing rapprochement between the design disciplines as they engage with the broader constellation of subjects that are imprecisely generalized as the social.

This essay examines recent interest in landscape as medium and model for urban design and the potential import of those developments for the discipline of urban planning. Until very recently, the decade-long disciplinary realignment between landscape architecture and urban design had prompted little response from the discipline of urban planning. This essay is provoked by the idea that urban planning has begun to be aware of the debates around landscape and urbanism that have been found productive for those concerned with the contemporary city[1]. If this assumption proves true, *New Geographies* could be well positioned to describe and disseminate those developments to multiple audiences.

Over the past decade the subject of landscape has enjoyed a renaissance within design culture. This well-documented resurgence of what had been described by some as a relatively moribund field of intellectual inquiry has been variously characterized as a recovery or renewal, and has been particularly fruitful for discussions of contemporary urbanism. Among the questions implied within the editorial frame of *New Geographies*

New Geographies Roundtable, Spring 2008

is the import of landscape's newfound ascendancy for the disciplines of geography and planning. In addition to its relevance for describing the contemporary urban field, might landscape have potential to resonate with the larger territorial subjects of urban planning? Ironically, the most compelling argument in this regard suggests that the potential for landscape to inform planning comes from its heightened profile within design culture and the deployment of ecology as model or metaphor rather than through the longstanding historical project of ecologically informed regional planning. As this point is a potential source of confusion, and is likely to be a topic of debate, this essay offers a provisional reading of how landscape might profitably inform the present and future commitments of urban planning.

The recent recovery of landscape might be thought of in the first instance as the (belated) impact of postmodernism on the field. This reading suggests that an essentially modernist positivist discourse of the natural sciences has been supplanted, if not made redundant, by the notion of nature as a cultural construct. In that formulation, landscape architecture moves from a position of positivist certainty over the mechanisms of ecological function to the culturally relativist position of ecology as a model for understanding the complex interactions between nature and culture. Of course landscape's recent cultural relevance has itself to do with a unique combination of broad environmental awareness in mass culture and the rise of the donor class as the means through which design is defined as culture.

Landscape's relevance as model for contemporary urbanization was first suggested by European architects and urbanists describing the North American city. It has come to stand for a profound critique of the perceived failures of urban design to effectively respond to the spatial decentralization, neoliberal economic shifts, and environmental toxicity in those cities. Equally, it has come to promise an alternative to the reactionary cultural politics of traditional urban form, simultaneously offering a future for urbanism in which environmental health, social welfare, and cultural aspiration are no longer mutually exclusive. Although it may be true that landscape architects were not the first to make such claims, the discipline has mounted spirited support for this position as the field diversifies and grows in design literacy.

Over the past decade, as landscape architecture has reconceived itself, the discipline of urban design has been largely preoccupied with various mechanisms for propping up traditional urban form, and has until recently been relatively slow to appreciate the import that landscape would come to have in discussions of North American urban form. These developments are not unrelated to the rapprochement between the design disciplines. Equally, they have been informed by calls for interdisciplinarity with respect to the challenges of the contemporary city as well as in design education. In this context, urban planning has been slow to apprehend the import of landscape's newfound cultural relevance for discussions of urbanism.

In many ways, planning's relative immunity to these developments within landscape architecture is not surprising given the history of the two disciplines. In the context of the cultural politics of the 1960s, or so goes the conventional narrative, many prominent planning departments (including those at Harvard University and the University of Toronto) left schools of architecture to articulate their own disciplinary identity and to distance themselves from the perceived hegemony of architecture among the design arts. Similarly, many departments of landscape architecture were radicalized on environmental issues and distanced themselves from the cultural and intellectual commitments of their architect colleagues. The combined effect was to alienate the design disciplines from one another, and to disengage architecture from the economic, ecological, and social contexts that had historically informed design. In that period of relative alienation between design culture and environmental activism, planning programs were predisposed to strike alliances with their environmentally minded colleagues in landscape architecture and to distance themselves from the seemingly subjective and self-referential commitments of the architecture discipline.

Although this brief historical sketch borders on caricature, it has come to enjoy the status of myth and continues to inform our understanding of the relationships between the design disciplines. As architecture, landscape architecture, and urban design have recently enjoyed a relative rapprochement, the question arises as to the relative impact of that renewed disciplinary proximity on planning. Asked another way: what is the current status of planning vis-à-vis these transformations? With respect to increased calls for interdisciplinarity in design culture and education? With respect to geography's current relevance for the discourse of landscape? With respect to landscape's emergence as medium and model of urban design? With respect to contemporary understandings of ecology?

One approach to these questions would be to examine the current paradigms and discourse available within urban planning. Recent literature suggests that the present moment in planning might be summarized in three historic oppositions. The first of these concerns top-down executive authority versus bottom-up organic community decision making. A second supposes an opposition between planning allied with design culture, as opposed to an organic vernacular. A third presupposes an ongoing opposition between planning as an instrument of the welfare state informed by environmental science and planning as realpolitik facilitator of laissez-faire economic development and the art of the deal. Although these facile oppositions are surely reductive, they continue to inform the discourse of planning, perpetuating a return to the political context of the 1960s in which they were formalized.[2]

1 Although the evidence is still circumstantial, it includes the fact that the 100th Annual Planning Conference of the American Planning Association (Las Vegas, April 26–May 1, 2008) dedicated a specific session to the topic of landscape as a medium of urbanization. As further evidence, in recent years several doctoral candidates in urban planning have taken up topics at the intersection of landscape and urbanism as the focus of their doctoral dissertations. Also relevant to this discussion are the range of academic institutions recently launching faculty searches in this area or augmenting their academic programs on these subjects. These include Harvard University's Graduate School of Design, MIT's Department of Urban Studies and Planning, the University of Pennsylvania's Design School, and the University of Toronto's Cities Centre.
2 This gloss of the current paradigms available to planning has been summarized in *Harvard Design Magazine*, no. 22, "Urban Planning Now: What Works, What Doesn't?" (Spring/Summer 2005); and in the corresponding *Harvard Design Magazine Reader*, no. 3, Urban Planning Today, William S. Saunders, ed. (Minneapolis: University of Minnesota Press), 2006.

New Geographies: Design, Agency, Territory

Neyran Turan, editor-in-chief

Journal, Issue 0, April 2008 **Editors:** Gareth Doherty, Rania Ghosn, El Hadi Jazairy, Antonio Petrov, Stephen J. Ramos. **Advisors:** Mohsen Mostafavi, Antoine Picon, Hashim Sarkis, Charles Waldheim. **Editorial Advisor:** Melissa Vaughn. **Graphic Design:** Wilcox Design. **Support:** The Aga Khan Program at the Harvard GSD.

New Geographies aims to examine the emergence of the geographic, a new but for the most part latent paradigm in design today—to articulate it and bring it to bear effectively on the social role of design.

After more than two decades of seeing architecture and urbanism as the spatial manifestation of the effects of globalization, it is time to consider the expanded agency of the designer. Designers are increasingly being compelled to shape larger scales and contexts, to address questions related to infrastructural problems, urban and ecological systems, and cultural and regional issues. These questions—previously confined to the domains of engineering, ecology, advertising, or regional planning—now require articulation through design. Encouraging designers to reexamine their tools and develop strategies to link attributes that had been understood to be either separate from each other or external to the design disciplines, those questions have also opened up a range of technical, formal, and social repertoires for architecture. Although in the past decade different versions of landscape and infrastructural urbanism have emerged in response to similar challenges, this new condition we call "the geographic" points to more than a shift in scale. As the synthesizing role that geography aspired to play among the physical, the economic, and the sociopolitical is now being increasingly shared by design, the need to articulate the geographic paradigm in design becomes urgent.

As much of the analysis in architecture, landscape, and urbanism—of emergent urban mutations and global changes on the spatial dimension—comes by way of social anthropology, human geography, and economics, the journal aims to extend these arguments by asking how the design practices can have a more active and transformative impact on the forces that shape contemporary urban realities. With attention to the delicate relation between the physical and the social, the form and the context, the very large and the very small, *New Geographies* will explore the formal repertoire of architecture and the agency of the designer within the wider contexts that produce the built environment. Through critical essays and design projects, the journal aims to open up discussions on the expanded role of the designer, with an emphasis on disciplinary repositionings as well as new attitudes.

New Geographies Roundtable, Spring 2008

TAICHUNG GATEWAY PROJECT:

A NEW SYNTHESIS OF PARK AND CITY   STAN ALLEN

Urbanism today is much talked about but little practiced. Architects are more fascinated than ever with big cities, but at a time of explosive urban growth, architects are less and less able to control the form of the city. Urbanization today is not only a global phenomenon of physical and cultural restructuring, but it has itself become a spatial effect of the distributed networks of communication, resources, finance, and migration that characterize contemporary life. The city today is everywhere and nowhere.

The disciplines of architecture, planning, and design have yet to devise effective techniques to manage the form and structure of the city, and they remain split between an avant-gardism that celebrates the anarchy of the contemporary city, and traditionalism that wants to impose known patterns of order over this wildly proliferating diversity. New Urbanists work closely with developers to build largely on ex-urban sites, but they have yet to produce a convincing urbanism. New towns are built from scratch in Asia and the Middle East, but these too lack the density, diversity, and complexity of the city. The emergence of landscape urbanism is a promising development, but its actual products have been limited to park-like interventions that leave the city more or less untouched.

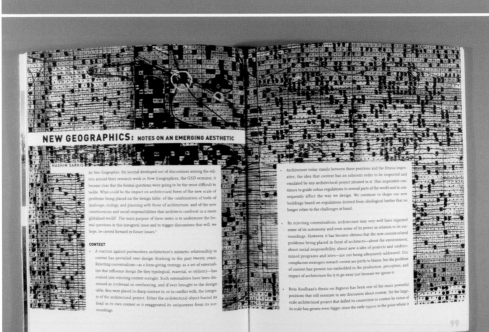

NEW GEOGRAPHICS: NOTES ON AN EMERGING AESTHETIC

HASHIM SARKIS

As *New Geographics*, the journal developed out of discussions among the editors around their research work in New Geographies, the GSD seminar, it became clear that the formal questions were going to be the most difficult to tackle. What could be the impact on architectural form of the new scale of problems being placed on the design table, of the combination of tools of landscape, ecology, and planning with those of architecture, and of the new constituencies and social responsibilities that architects confront in a more globalized world? The main purpose of these notes is to underscore the formal questions in this inaugural issue and to trigger discussions that will, we hope, be carried forward in future issues.

CONTEXT

• A reaction against postmodern architecture's mimetic relationship to context has prevailed over design thinking in the past twenty years. Rejecting contextualism—as a form-giving strategy, as a set of externalities that influence design (be they typological, material, or stylistic)—has evolved into rejecting context outright. Such externalities have been dismissed as irrelevant or overbearing, and if ever brought to the design table, they were placed in sharp contrast to, or in conflict with, the integrity of the architectural project. Either the architectural object buried its head in its own context or it exaggerated its uniqueness from its surroundings.

• Architecture today stands between these positions and the fitness imperative, the idea that context has an inherent order to be respected and emulated by any architectural project situated in it. This imperative continues to guide urban regulations in several parts of the world and to consequently affect the way we design. We continue to shape our new buildings based on regulations derived from ideological battles that no longer relate to the challenges at hand.

• By rejecting contextualism, architecture may very well have regained some of its autonomy and even some of its power in relation to its surroundings. However, it has become obvious that the new context-related problems being placed in front of architects—about the environment, about social responsibility, about new scales of projects and undetermined programs and sites—are not being adequately addressed. Our complacent strategies toward context are partly to blame, but the problem of context has proven too embedded in the production, perception, and impact of architecture for it to go away just because we ignore it.

• Rem Koolhaas's thesis on Bigness has been one of the more powerful positions that still resonate in any discussion about context. Yet the large-scale architectural project that defied its connection to context by virtue of its scale has grown even bigger since the early 1990s, to the point where it

The Architecture of Geography: Istanbul, Mixed-Use Development, and the Panoramic Condition

Hashim Sarkis

Options Studio, Fall 2007 **Students:** Abdulatif Almishari, Jennifer Bonner, Christine Canabou, Miaoyan Huang, Soe Won Hwang, Min Ter Lim, Olga Orchakova, Maja Paklar, Sangwook Park, Mazen Sakr, Juliana Silbermins, Michael Sypkens. **Teaching Assistant:** Mete Sonmez. **Sponsor:** The Aga Khan Program at the Harvard GSD. **Collaboration:** Bilgi University, Istanbul.

The studio explored the urban and architectural potentials of mixed-use development as it attains exponentially larger sizes and costs. Both theoretical projections about scale (theories of bigness, of compactness, etc.) and the corporate models that have been adopted for such large-scale developments in the past ten years (e.g., Emirates Towers in Dubai, Petronas Center in Kuala Lumpur) have proven inadequate in the face of this new scale of development and its potentials. Even the expressive or iconic aspects of these developments (two towers on a base, corporate identity suppressing the expression of mixture) have begun to show signs of fatigue.
The studio focused specifically on the geographic dimension of this new scale of development, and the ability of urban architecture to reshape its larger context in a positive way.

The setting of Istanbul was particularly important for this exploration. The arrival of a new scale of mixed-use development to the city in the 1990s shifted its business center to the northern areas of Maslak and Etiler and created new habits of working and living, further aggravating its traffic problems, and most importantly, radically transforming its historically protected skyline. The heavy bases of these developments disrupted the fabric of the city and block visibility, and the tall towers they supported challenged the horizontal geography of the city's panorama. The studio explored the formal potentials of this horizontal geography as it manifested itself programmatically and visually.

Over the past twenty years, large-scale urban development has grown to match the size of real estate investments and has become increasingly mixed in program, catering to the demand for the flexibilization of uses on the part of developers.
The mixture of uses has generated provocative theories in architecture and urban design, but rarely have these speculations led to anything more than the celebration and intensification of the isolation of mixed-use projects from their context, and to separation among the different components of these large-scale developments.

The studio examined these phenomena and the projections about their future. It also looked at some of the more challenging theoretical positions such as those of Rem Koolhaas, Abalos and Herreros, and Luis Fernandez-Galiano. Benefiting from the increasing scale, population, and urban impact of mixed-use development, the studio explored the potential of heightening the mixing and the urban dimensions of such projects.

Michael Sypkens

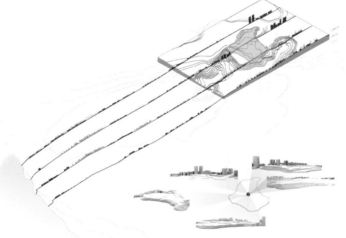

Maja Paklar

Mazen Sakr

Min Ter Lim

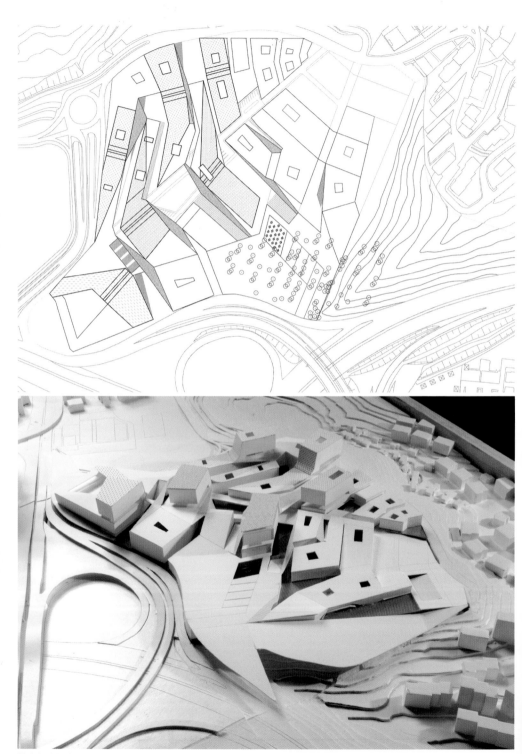

Abdulatif Almishari

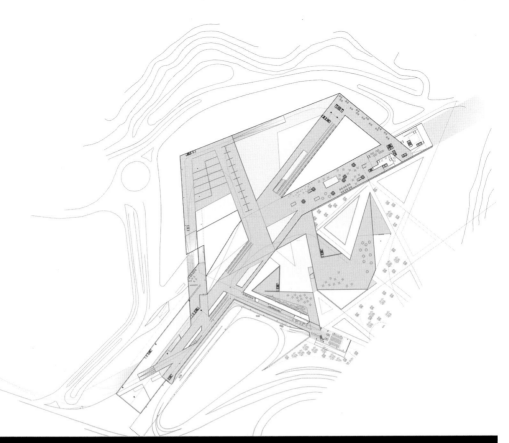

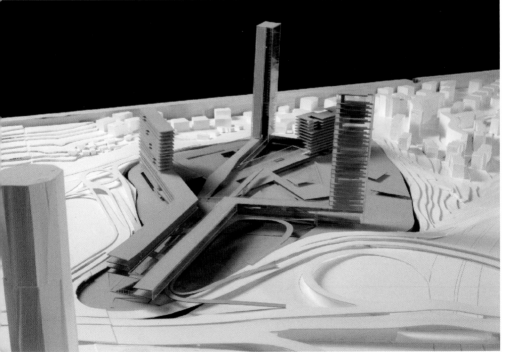

Mazen Sakr

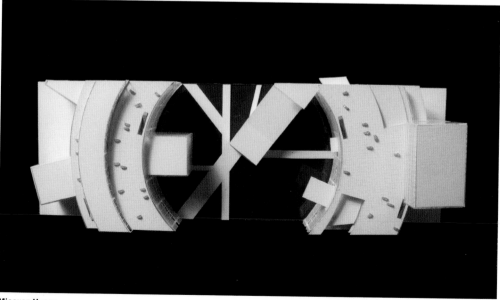

Miaoyan Huang

The Tenth Aga Khan Award Cycle

Homi Bhabha
Lecture, April 2, 2008

Faced with the wealth of architectural intelligence and the weight of expertise present in the room, staring back at me this evening, my presence at the podium can only be explained as an act of charity and hospitality. In his contribution to the exhibition catalog, Dean Mostafavi characterizes the traditional Islamic society as "a space of hospitality and public encounter," and it is in that spirit of shared hospitality that I address you this evening. For what is hospitality if it cannot accommodate the unexpected guest, the unlikely man who comes to dinner, and, if I may mix my metaphors, sets the cat amongst the pigeons? This act of hospitality does, however, reflect a deeper truth about the symbolic vision represented by the award. The award extends a generous transnational hospitality across the Muslim world, spanning a plurality of communities and continents.

His Highness, the Aga Khan, elevated the ethic of inquiry and interrogation above all others when he spoke to us in Kuala Lumpur last summer. Question, he said, always question. And true hospitality, a virtue that mixes freedom with solidarity, independence with integration, is always open to crossing the threshold of thought, open to traversing the territories of tradition, open to the next question, and open to the new horizon. It is this ethic of hospitality in matters relating to landscape, public space and the built environment that I vividly recall as being the defining quality of my experience as a member of the jury. We aspired toward the goals of social inclusion and cultural integration as the foundation of the built environment. We attempted to advance a sense of building—and of belonging—enhanced by an open dialogue that resulted from a transparent process of negotiation, interlocution, and construction. In serving to enhance architectural innovation in Muslim societies, the jurisdiction of the award includes Muslim nation-states but goes beyond them—well beyond them—to recognize societies that are part of the global Muslim diaspora across the world.

This has important territorial, temporal, and cultural consequences. The award reaches beyond the territorial concept of the sovereignty of nationness—or national citizenship—to reach out to the transnational experience of minorities, of migration—and indeed of social marginalization—that has a history that far precedes contemporary globalization. Going beyond the jurisdiction of territoriality made us particularly attentive to the effect of political divisions and spatial partitions inflicted upon neighborly community. The rehabilitation of the walled city of Nicosia, for instance, aspires towards eliminating the buffer zone that divides Greek Cypriots from Turkish Cypriots, in order to facilitate freedom of movement and a civic life between both communities with the hope of a more inclusive and integrated civility and polity established in the future.

The award does not participate in polarizing historical temporalities that pit traditionalism against modernity in order to impose a hegemonic norm or style of contemporaneity across the globe. The rehabilitation of Shibam is a case in point. It entailed both the reconstruction of contemporary infrastructural necessities, like the sewage system, as well as the reengineering of the traditional practices of mud architecture through the agency of local master builders, their apprentices, and organizations.

Tenth Aga Khan Award exhibition, Spring 2008

And finally, the award does not discriminate harshly between spiritualism and secularism, between politics and faith. And it keeps open the possibility of a more inclusive and integrated vision of social or subjective transformation in which the transport between articles of political faith and spiritual belief might constitute a third space that borders on both the secular and the sacred, without belonging only to either. Such a mission is achieved, for instance, in that sublime space, the Samir Kassir Square, that opens up a busy street in Beirut to the possibilities of meditative experiences, as well as the memories of political and intellectual martyrs. The two ficus trees that mark this spot are indomitable survivors of the civil war, 1975 to 1990, outlasting the experience of trauma and violence, as if at last nature speaks truth to history in the same gesture as an urban landscape heals an unsettled city.

The Aga Khan award reflects the changing world of Muslim realities that transforms the global *ummah*. A shift in vocabulary from Muslim societies to Muslim realities reflects the way we live today as part of an intercultural, multi-faith world, crossing cultural boundaries and national borders. We live in the midst of difficult transitions in custom and belief, and complicated transvaluations of identity and social life. Transition and translation are complex states of being that constitute the culture of everyday life. In a state of transition or translation, you are caught often in a state of anxiety, of ambivalence, between identifying with an establishing community of one's origins and traditions, while having at the same time to relate to an empowering community that provides you with new, revisionary values and identifications.

"Establishing" and "empowering" are only approximate, unfixed terms of personal and social reference. I have named them thus in order to reflect the commonly held view that for all of us, some form of tradition imparts a sense of continuity, while empowerment is an invitation to experiment with newer self-identifications and emergent, experimental beliefs and collective values. This dynamic of the established and the empowering is as true of the diasporic conditions of migration as it is of the transformation in the indigenous lives of those who stay at home. The one dynamic works in the other direction, too. No individual group or society experiences social transition or cultural translation in neatly polarized parcels of contrasting views or contradictory values, *pace* the "clash of civilizations" thesis, which has a certain currency in parts of this campus.

This is because the conflict or the coexistence of diverse cultural genealogies is continually in a state of translation, even if the relations between its members are antagonistic. The prevalence of intergenerational conflict that reshapes cultural values within a single family or community is also in a process of transition and translation. And this creates lifeworlds which we all experience as asymmetrical, historically contingent, and often morally puzzling.

Many of the submissions for the Tenth Awards Cycle occupy this problematic but productive terrain in between our understanding of traditional, established Muslim societies and beliefs, and displaced, empowering Muslim reality. Change and challenging circumstances are, of course, part of both worlds. But the composition of what we experience as our contemporaneity, the speed of transformation, the conflict of values, the intensity and contingency of identities and solidarities in transition, these are part and parcel of a process of change that may be integrated and calibrated in different ways.

The bridge between Muslim societies and Muslim realities—as indeed with other communities—is at times a bridge over troubled waters. It was our privilege as members of the master jury to be faced with architectural projects that raised important issues about an *ummah* that is democratic and dialogical, and maps both worlds, not by sitting on the fence, but by moving vigorously between conflicting spaces, values, ideas, and times. How should we evaluate a new housing scheme whose disposition of spaces harmoniously and homogenously accommodates a sect that is governed by strict rules of power and masculinist authority? Does architectural excellence allow us to judge what may, or may not, be considered the good life amongst different communities? These questions, posed by the material and constructional practices of architecture with a remarkable concreteness and visibility, enable us to reflect on complex issues of scale in the midst of a veritable Babel of celebratory voices that hail the infinite, almost Leviathan extensionality and expandability of the global condition.

As a jury, we were challenged to keep adjusting our critical and conceptual lenses as we moved across the varied landscapes of the *ummah* and its architectural artifacts and practices. A market town in a small, countryside part of Burkina Faso becomes the model for a constellation of similar markets across the region. A school in Bangladesh that could be reproduced at low cost in other inaccessible, poor regions. Sewer systems in the dense urban conditions of ancient cities in Yemen. The Dutch Embassy in Ethiopia, which is a collaboration between Dutch and Ethiopian expertise. A small reflecting water garden in Beirut, located on an axis that gives the narrow site a deep, contemplative scale much larger than the ground on which it is built.

Scale is not merely a problem internal to architectural knowledge or practice. The scale of the contemporary Muslim world reveals profound differences in sites and localities. Rural communities, small towns, industrial cities, private homes, public institutions, that demand imagination in design and practical interventions. Scale is indeed an architectural innovation that both responds to site specificity, while creating or constructing at the same time a sense of locality, locality which is never simply a naturalistic, *a priori* reality. In that sense, scale is also an issue of the ethics of architecture. What one chooses to build, who one chooses to build for, where the building intervention is made, with whom one collaborates, the values that the building represents in itself, and in relation to others.

A different kind of lens snapped into place when we took up the question of conservation and restoration, which are all, after all, issues of the time scale of the built environment. Conservation and restoration are often thought of as processes of pickling the past in the present, and fetishizing the aura of antiquity. But if you approach these issues from the perspective of cultural translation, as I have suggested, premised on the ongoing presence of the past in the present, rather than the polarities of tradition versus modernity, then conservation and restoration become our commitment to keeping alive the future-directed hopefulness of history. And it is this hopefulness of history that marks the huge energy of the Aga Khan award process. Conservation and restoration are not about asserting the permanence of the past, but emphasizing their productive contribution to the future. The life span of materials that constitute ancient monuments argues against the notion of preservation, because as materials decay, they have to be recreated in the present. Technological skills must be relearned and re-taught to new generations of craftsmen. New chemicals and engineering techniques are invented in relation to past techniques, in a revisionary structure, in a revisionary world, in order to rebuild the edifice. Restoration is always a work in progress or, in the preferred words of our jury, a work in process. But so is human history and the narrative of each individual life. The revisionary emphasis of restoration and conservation shares a dynamic relation to the past, which is visible in contemporary projects. For instance, two young Singaporean architects recreate the traditional monsoon window for a modern apartment building that consequently becomes less dependent on air conditioning, and lightens the load on an already overburdened electricity grid.

Scale, then, represents an architectural and ethical commitment to what Wittgenstein, in his scattered notes on architecture, described as not constructing a building, as much as in having a perspicuous view of the foundations of possible buildings. Conservation or restoration, I have argued, are not about the past, but about the continuing pressure in the presence of a hope for the future, and a particular thoughtfulness about the forward reach of the present. In this sequence of architectural hopefulness, there is no responsibility to the environment as important to the commitment to sustainability. For sustainability tests the grandiosity of our ambitions against the available and appropriate scale of natural resources. How suitable are our schemes for this particular lay of land, for this specific climate, for this artifactual need or human interest? As the best of our nominations readily persuaded us, sustainability is about creating environments committed to survival and well being that are intolerant of authoritarian claims to sovereignty and inhospitable assumptions of cultural or civilizational supremacy.

Wittgenstein thinks through architecture to give abstract thought a concrete quality that renders more visible its worldly implications and its cultural values, the perspicuity of foundational thinking, or the tectonic worlds—to borrow Hashim Sarkis' phrase—that combine the arts of construction with the craftsmanship of everyday custom and everyday life. The use of an architectural metaphor for conceptual modeling in the work of Wittgenstein bears a resemblance to the mobility of computer-generated graphics that display difficult dimensions and awkward angles that are inaccessible to the naked eye and invisible to the linear logic of arguments. If good architecture expresses a thought, as Wittgenstein argues, then good thinking is enhanced by the use of the appropriate architectural metaphor, conceived in the concept of the detail, which is central to the exhibition here this evening.

Wittgenstein, as you know, was obsessed by the clarity of the design as a whole, and in particular, by the way in which the details of the house—doorknobs, windows, window locks, screens, and radiators—express the essential idea of the whole construction. But there is, I believe, another sense in which such details are components of human social interaction. A doorknob immediately implies the hand that turns it and the eye that takes in the space that flows beyond the door. The window brings air into the house and breathes in the light. The screen is the skin that defines inside and outside, sometimes night and day, keeping them separate, or allowing them to negotiate each other in the erotic, crepuscular encounter of twilight.

oesn't a focus on detail scale down the ambition of architectural achievement and lower
ıe lofty standards demanded of one of the world's most prestigious architectural awards?
hould we be looking for details, however significant or symbolic, when the global
xpansion of the *ummah* demands that we think in large, capacious ways that propose uni-
ərsal frames of reference? I don't believe so. Working with detail makes you aware of the
adequacy of the vocabularies of volume or dimension, large and little, big and small,
representing the complexity of cultural construction and cultural comparison. In a world
 increasingly transnational cultural traffic, the signature of specificity and locality,
ıe productive signs of social difference, often inhere in the telling detail that signifies the
tersection between value systems and representational references. Scale is a measure of
omplexity, not size, and the detail is often a visible and concrete symptom of transition that
lows you to access to the larger structures of the transmission of plural traditions and the
hole world of transformation and then translation in the question of design.

our search for continuities or differences, across cultures, traditions, urban and rural
ontexts, we too hastily demand broad outlines, stark oppositions, large frameworks,
 harmonious horizons. Too often, however, the subtle processes of cultural transition
ıd transmission happen at the site of the moments of overlap of the moment of the detail
ithin a larger pattern of thinking or dwelling, in the way in which the doorknob, for
Jittgenstein, is itself a symptom of the clarity of the vision of the plan itself. Something
most imperceptible emerges at the border or margins of cultural constructions, be they
uildings or books, and becomes the harbinger of what is emergent, what is new and
nnovative. This is the domain of the detail. As transformative patterns of thinking and
welling become visible in the interstices of past and present, the detail provides us with
 compass that points to new ways of living and building side by side with each other.

ood thinking demands both clarity of intention and precision of purpose in the execution
 a project, be it a building, a sculpture, or the drafting of a law. But such a project must be
ccompanied by a measure of ethical perspicuity in the planning and building process that
roposes a design for living, an architect's plan, an artist's vision, a politician's worldview,
hich then aspires to some version of the good life and contributes to the construction of
ie common good as a mode of habitation, a way of coming home. To find a home is not,
s the more complacent or comfortable phrase has it, to be at home. To be at home
aptures a moment of ontological security. It leads you to discovering that your originary
npulses, the foundational paradigms you sought, seem somehow to fall within the horizons
f your thinking and your mode of living. To find a home, contrarily, is to arrive after the tur-
ulence of journey and inquiry at a place of thought and belief that provides a perspective,
ven a theory or a concept, but no final conclusions, no *telos*. When these different notions
f home joyously overlap, you have a moment of epiphany. When they disastrously diverge
om each other, you experience a form of tragedy.

he ethic of hopefulness represented by the Aga Khan Architectural Award is committed
) asking the difficult question of what it means to build, and poses the complex thought
f what architecture can aspire to in the contemporary Muslim world, which is also the
ontemporary world, as we know it and share it in relation to other faiths and other inter-
ultural modes of dwelling. Located as we are somewhere on the road between being at
ome and striving to find a home, we find ourselves in that realm of question and question-
g which is where the birth of architecture takes place.

Preservation: Operations and Mechanisms

Defne Bozkurt, Landon Brown, Darren Chang, Dina Ge, Chris Parlato, Lisa Su, Lindsay Wai;
Rem Koolhaas, advisor

Independent Thesis, Fall 2007 **Teaching Associate:** Margaret Arbanas. **Assistance:** Toshiko Mori (Harvard GSD); Talia Dorsey; Anu Leinonen, Dongmei Yao (OMA); Els Silvrants (beiLAB); Dr. Ron Van Oers (UNESCO); Jorge Otero-Pailos; Ai Wei Wei; Han Yan (Urban China); Wang Jun; Hua Xinmin; Xie Li (ICOMOS China); He Shuzhong, Hu Xinyu (CHP); Huang Yan (Beijing Municipal Commission of Urban Planning); Zhu Wenyi (Tsing Hua University); Lu Zhou; Ou Ning; Zhu Pei.

As our energy reserves are depleting, so are our history's. In the last century, preservation has been eclipsed by a protective conservatism that, at its most perverse, no longer serves the authenticity of history but rather brokers claims to it. The fabricated modern reconstruction of Dresden city center now wields its UNESCO World Heritage status against any authentic modern construction in its vicinity. Considered antithetical to its mandate, contemporary architecture is excluded from preservation's domain. In kind, modern architectural discourse and practice have returned the snub. Ironically, the resulting confusion has created an insatiable appetite and production of the pseud historical—the pathological displacement of the modern architect's suppressed desire? Or the manifest form of the preservationist's blind assault on authenticity?

The subject of this research was to interrogate this relationship and suggest that within the authentic process of modern architectural production, the act and understanding of preservation is acutely integral. The work was organized as a collective research project divided into specific parts. It started by establishing a preliminary overview of the notion of preservation—its historical basis, its political position, its operative mechanisms, its scale(s) of operatio et al. The final work is as a comprehensive study of the phenomenon and mechanisms of preservation worldwide and a catalogue of case studies situated within this landscape.

In conjunction with the research an AMO/GSD collaboration investigated alternative preservation models for Beijing. The work was part of the Xisi-Bei Project International Invitation Exhibition in Beijing and was published in *Domus China*.

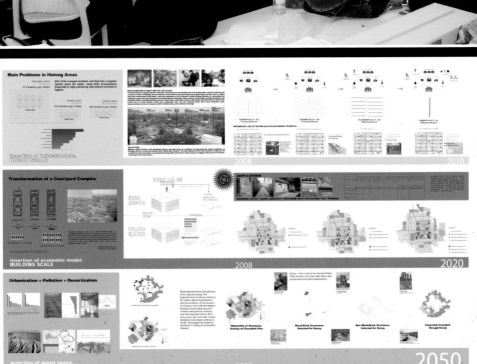

EVOLUTIONARY PRESERVATION

can preservation equal modernization through a model of controlled laissez faire?

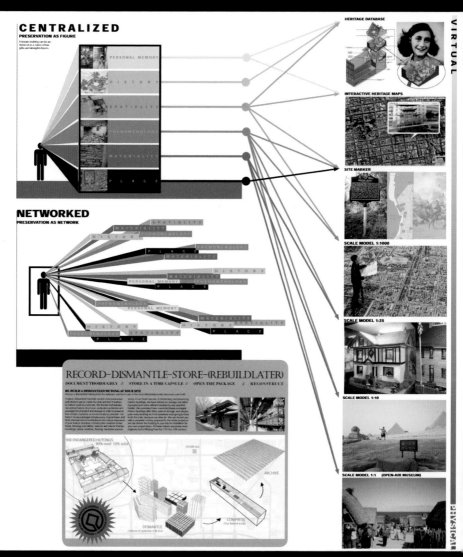

THE ARCHIVE
does the age of networked decentralization provide new models for the preservation (and definition) of authenticity?

HERITAGE PRESERVATION AS STRATIFICATION

CAN VERTICAL   CREATE
HERITAGE REPROGRAMMING

CAN VERTICAL HERITAGE THRESHOLDS GENERATE
DIRECT PROVISIONS FOR PRESERVATION SITES?
HERITAGE REFINANCING

WHAT ARE THE   SITES? CAN THEY
ABSORB VERTICAL DEVELOPMENT AND PRODUCTION?
HERITAGE TOWER BLOCKS

CAN THE RELATIONSHIP BETWEEN THE
AND THE   ESTABLISH THE 21ST C. HUTONG?
PRESERVATION CONSOLIDATION

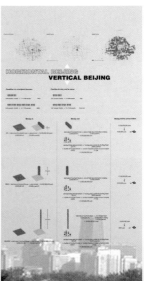

HORIZONTAL BEIJING
VERTICAL BEIJING

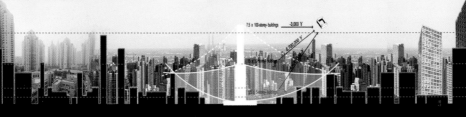

VERTICAL HERITAGE
how might planometric preservation serve to legislate vertical production?

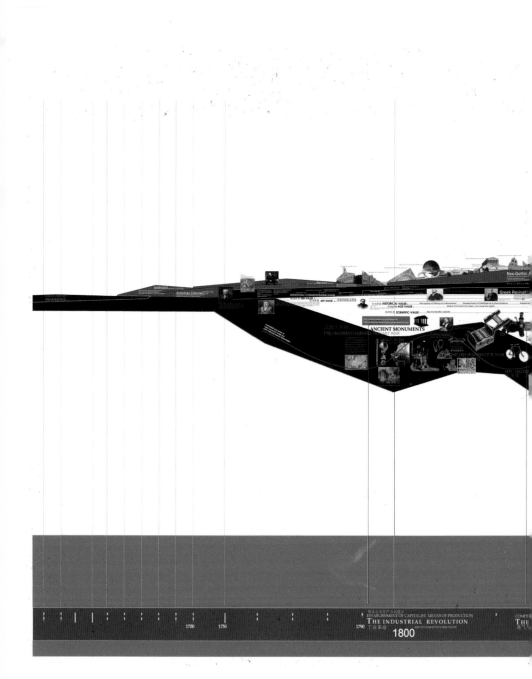

1

2

1 Finger Proposal: Natural and Anthropogenic Systems and Play

RED HOOK : ZONING / PHASING:

PHASE 2
Manufacturing X-1
Light industrial special mixed use districts
Attention to historic preservation
20 acres

PHASE 2
Residential 7
Commercial 1 Overlay
3.44 max F.A.R.; 240 d.u./acre max
5.5 acres + proposed development

PHASE 1
Residential 6A
Commercial 1 Overlay
3.0 F.A.R.; 190 d.u./ acre max.
29 acres

PHASE 1
Park Extension
Purchased by the city
13 acres

PHASE 3
Residential 6 with Commercial 3 Overlay
2.43 F.A.R.; 175 d.u./ acre max.
C3 allows for commercial maritime uses
13 acres

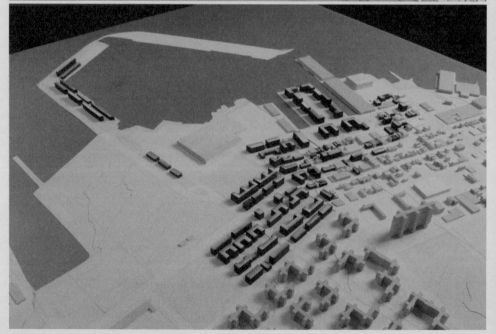

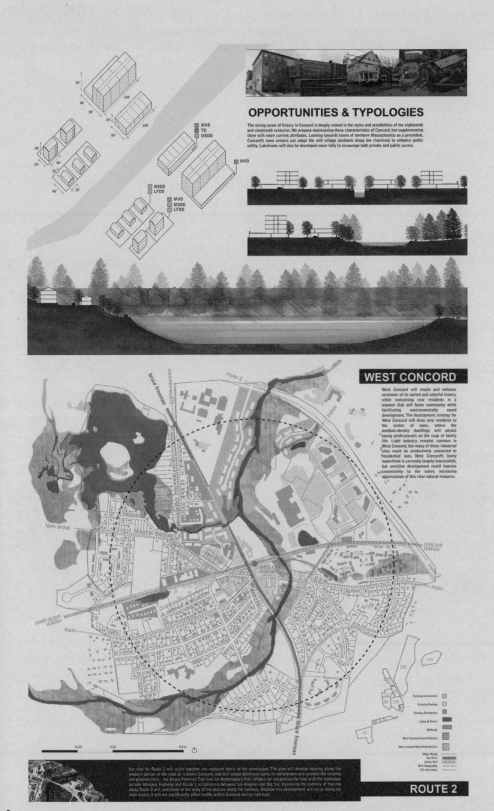

OPPORTUNITIES & TYPOLOGIES

The strong sense of history in Concord is deeply rooted in the styles and sensibilities of the eighteenth and nineteenth centuries. We propose maintaining these characteristics of Concord, but supplementing them with more current attributes. Looking towards towns of northern Massachusetts as a precedent, Concord's town centers can adopt the mill village aesthetic along the riverfront to enhance public utility. Lakefronts will also be developed more fully to encourage both private and public access.

WEST CONCORD

West Concord will retain and enhance remnants of its varied and colorful history, while welcoming new residents in a manner that will foster community while facilitating environmentally sound development. The development strategy for West Concord will draw new residents to the center of town, where the medium-density dwellings will attract young professionals on the cusp of family life. Light industry remains common in West Concord, but many of these industrial sites could be productively converted to residential uses. West Concord's lovely waterfront is currently largely inaccessible, but sensitive development could improve connectivity to the water, increasing appreciation of this vital natural resource.

Our plan for Route 2 will stitch together the ruptured fabric of the streetscape. The plan will develop housing along the western portion of the road as it enters Concord, and will create additional paths to complement and connect the existing and planned trails – the Bruce Freeman Trail and the Reformatory Trail. Models for integrating the road with the landscape include Montauk Highway and Route 1 in California between Los Angeles and Big Sur. Increasing the quantity of housing along Route 2 will contribute to the unity of the texture along the roadway. Because this development will occur along the main artery, it will not significantly affect traffic within Concord during rush hour.

ROUTE 2

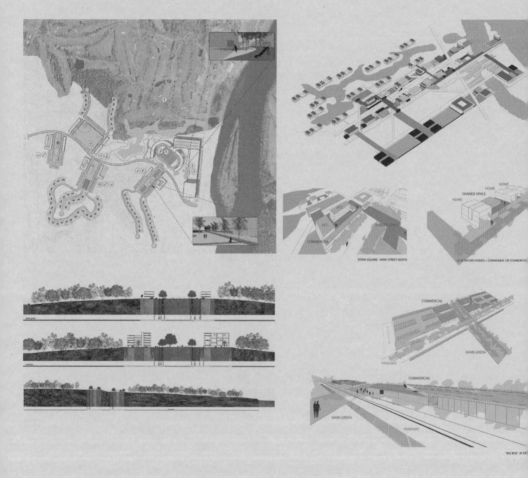

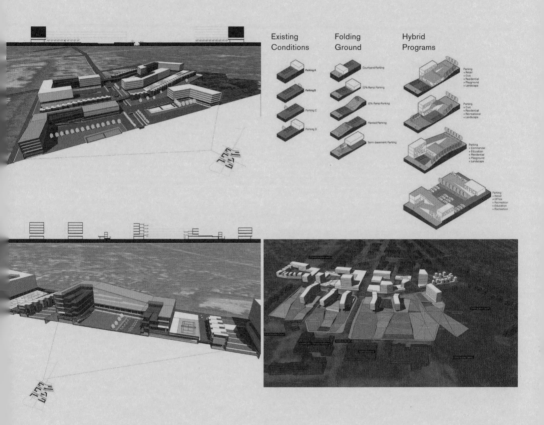

Existing
Conditions

Folding
Ground

Hybrid
Programs

Technology

Critical Digital: What Matter(s)?

Kostas Terzidis, organizer
Conference, April 18–19, 2008 Moderators: Jock Herron, Mariana Ibáñez, Jan Jungclauss, Jeanette Kuo, Nashid Nabian, Taro Narahara, Ingeborg Rocker, Teri Rueb, Kostas Terzidis, Zenovia Toloudi, Dido Tsigaridi. Participants: Yehuda E. Kalay (University of California), Bob Giddings, Margaret Horne (Northumbria University), Dominik Holzer (RMIT University), Anastasia Karandinou, Leonidas Koutsoumpos, Richard Coyne (University of Edinburgh), Paolo Fiamma (University of Pisa), Tim Schork (RMIT University), Tomasz Jaskiewicz (TU Delft), Onur Yüce Gün (KPF New York), Jonas Coersmeier (Büro / Pratt Institute), David Celento, Del Harrow (The Pennsylvania State University), Emmanouil Vermisso (ArchitRecture), Sherif Abdelmohsen (Georgia Institute of Technology), Oliver Neumann (University of British Columbia), David Harrison, Michael Donn (Victoria University of Wellington), Christian Friedrich (TU Delft), Theodoros Dounas (Aristoteleio University of Thessaloniki), Panagiotis Parthenios (Harvard GSD), Jack Breen (TU Delft), Julian Breen (Utrecht University), Daniel Cardoso Llach (MIT), Branko Kolarevic (University of Calgary), Ingeborg Rocker (Harvard GSD), Katerina Tryfonidou, Dimitris Gourdoukis (Washington University in St. Louis, Greece), Sawako Kaijima, Panagiotis Michalatos (Adams Kara Taylor), Aya Okabe, Tsukasa Takenaka, Jerzy Wojtowicz (University of British Columbia), Orkan Telhan (MIT), Bernhard Sommer (TU Delft), Josh Lobel (MIT), Serdar Asut (Anadolu University), Jerry Laiserin (The LaiserinLetter), Yanni Loukissas (MIT), Simon Y. Kim (MIT), Mariana Ibanez (Harvard GSD), Edgardo Perez Maldonado (University of Puerto Rico), Francisca M. Rojas, Kristian Kloeckl, Carlo Ratti (MIT), Ole B. Jensen (Aalborg University), Greg More (RMIT University), Joseph B. Juhász, Robert H. Flanagan (University of Colorado), Jock Herron, (Harvard GSD), Dimitris Papanikolaou (MIT), Rodrigo Martin Quijada (University of Santiago de Chile), Sergio Araya (MIT), Sotirios D. Kotsopoulos (MIT), Magdalini Eleni Pantazi (MIT), Anthony Burke (Sydney University of Technology), Mahesh Senagala (UT San Antonio), Erik Conrad (Concordia University), Lydia Kallipoliti (Princeton University), Alexandros Tsamis (MIT), Neri Oxman (MIT), Sha Xin Wei (Concordia University).

Critical Digital aims to challenge the basis of contemporary digital media arguments and foster a dialogue about digital media, technology, and design, in order to identify, distinguish, and offer a critique on current trends, tendencies, movements, and practices in digital culture. Critical Digital provides a forum for discussion and enrichment of this discourse through diverse activities, symposia, competitions, conferences, and publications to support dialogue that challenges what is rapidly becoming the de facto mainstream. What is digital? Why should design be digital (or not)? How have practitioners and schools been using digital media?

The first Critical Digital conference was titled What Matter(s)?. As digital phenomena seems to elude the current theoretical discourse in architecture, a critical discussion is emerging as a means to address, understand, clarify, and assess the elusive nature of this discourse. Issues related to virtuality, ephemerality, continuity, materiality, or ubiquity, while originally invented to explain digital or computational phenomena, are used today in the context of a still material-based design. What is the nature of their use? Is materiality subject to abstract digital concepts? Is the digital buildable? What "matters?" As we progress to design for the built environment, interactive space, and the body, what materializations are actually emerging? What physical manifestations and manifestos are to be promoted?

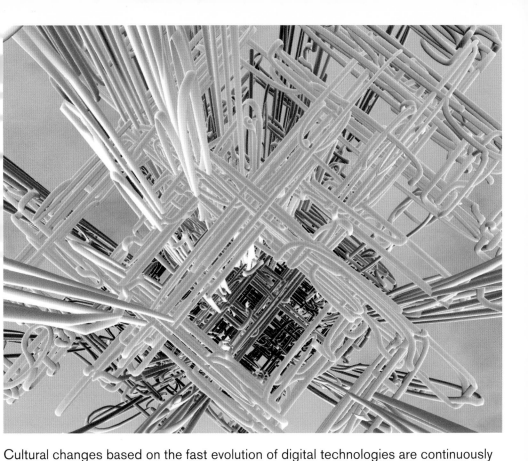

Cultural changes based on the fast evolution of digital technologies are continuously developing and affecting our activities as professionals, academics, and citizens. Digital culture has affected our notions as inhabitants and creators of a built environment, changing and affecting the way we conceive, transform, and produce space. Digital design and production processes are simulating and integrating material and environmental conditions, while addressing innovative methods of conception and realization of ideas at all scales. This has opened rich areas of research and important cross-pollinations and multidisciplinary approaches that reinforce and expand the connections between practitioners, industry, and academia. A challenge to creativity, rigor, and exploration, these processes are also a product of an increasingly complex understanding of what design is, what designers can produce, and their relation to the material and physical conditions of the built environment. It is fundamental to understand how the development of digitally enhanced products and spaces is affecting our experience at all scales. New relationships and methods of communication imply new models of interaction with the built environment, mediated through digital devices and embedded computation. These new relationships call for a critical and multidisciplinary approach to design that can engage the complex phenomena and fast development of technology without losing sight of what matters: the substance.

Versioning: Architecture as Series
Ingeborg Rocker

The introduction of computation has allowed for the visualization of mathematical calculations which were for a long time simply too complex. Today, the differential calculus underlying most interactive 3D modeling software has informed the shift from an architecture of modularity towards an architecture of seriality and design versions. Versioning exceeds simple variation between different parameterized design iterations to operate at the micro-scale, within the structure and aesthetic of digital design itself.

Tempus Fugit:
Transitions and Performance in Architecture
Simon Y. Kim (MIT), Mariana Ibáñez

Architecture is a one-directional flow of information: the building is an inert object, whose physicality is static, from which meaning is derived. Even in process-driven design, the synthesis of the many and the ordered is evident in the materiality of the architectural manifestation: buildings presented as a result of process cannot be separated from the reading of their generative operations. Rather than constructing meaning through coding (joining a concept to an object) or instantiation (one version from a larger field of possibilities), a time-based dialectic that is bidirectional, or even multinodal, can continually self-renew its meaning and material configuration through the active participation of the occupant.

Analog versus Digital: Why Bother?
The Role of Critical Points of Change (CPCs) as a Vital Mechanism for Enhancing Design Ability
Panagiotis Parthenios

Critical Points for Change (CPCs) are crucial moments when the architect suddenly becomes able to "see" something which drives him/her to go back and either alter an idea and refine it, or reject it and pursue a new one. Crucial parts of the design process, they are a vital mechanism for enhancing design. The right choice and combination of multiple design tools, analog and digital, allows the designer to overcome the influences and limitations imposed by a single tool, in a design landscape illustrated by coexistence, complementing, and evolution.

Shaping the Global City: The Digital Culture of Markets, Norbert Wiener, and the Musings of Archigram
Jock Herron

The contemporary built environment is increasingly generated using powerful computational tools that are shaping the "digital culture" of design. The primary shaper of global cities today, however, is another "digital culture," one defined by the confluence of professions and institutions that constitute our global financial markets. The prescient insights of Archigram into the cybernetic future of cities, the spatial implications of nomadic "digitized" capital, and the hazards of desensitizing and dematerializing the professional practices of design and finance reveals the connection and common origins of these two cultures.

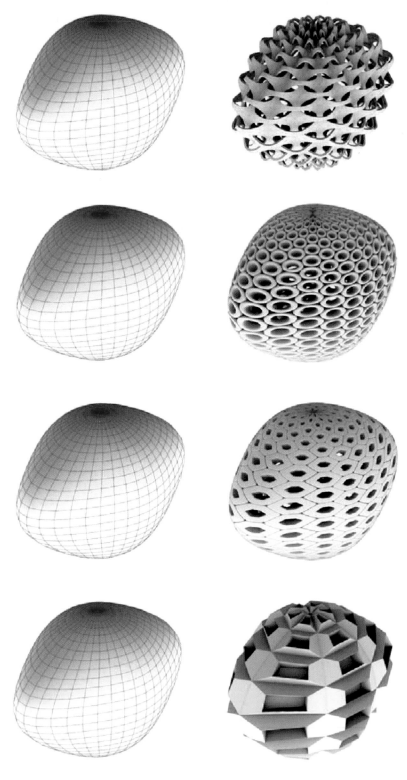

Ingeborg Rocker, versioning model studies

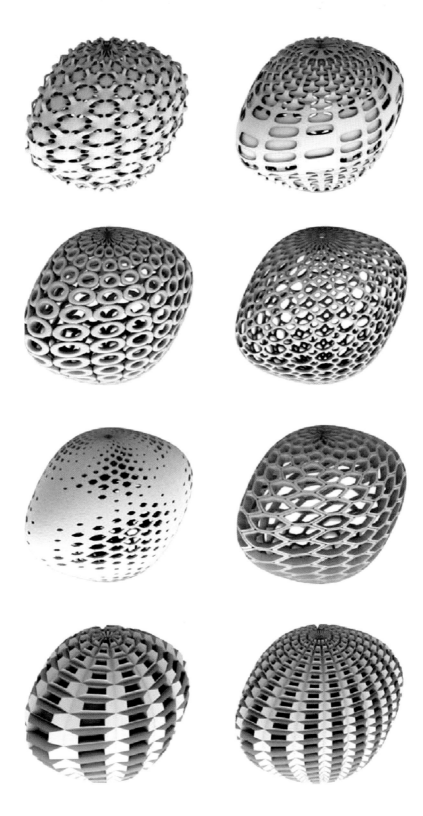

Construction Automation

Martin Bechthold

Seminar, Spring 2008 Students: Keith Coleman, Katherine Foreman, Maciej Kaczynski, Anthony Kane, Taro Narahara, Gregory Spaw.

The seminar introduced students to emerging technologies under the broad umbrella of construction automation. As an extension of research on computer-aided design and manufacturing techniques, the seminar introduced the principles of robotics and automated systems in the context of architectural construction, with reference to product design and other industries. Topics included a historical overview as well as an introduction to different types of robotic systems, automation systems and their elements. Techniques and strategies for programming industrial robots were introduced, with an emphasis on the use of offline simulation and programming environments with graphical user interfaces. Distinctions between numerically-controlled machines and robotic systems were made throughout.

After researching case studies of applications and advanced technologies, students developed and conducted immersion experiments with actual industrial robots and their associated programming and teaching environment. Experimental work explored "design for robotics" for both on-site and off-site applications. How is design and construction impacted by the introduction of automated, robotic systems? Projects ranged from problem-solving to work that was highly speculative in nature, encouraging the speculative and creative use of robotic material handling and fabrication.

Robotic assembly studies

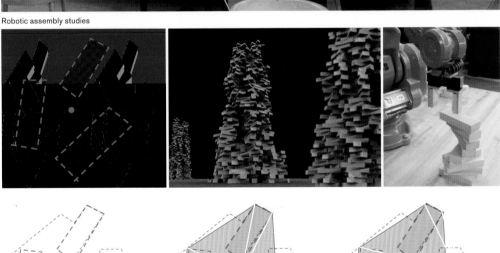

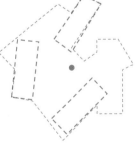

Center of mass

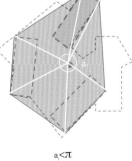

$a_i < \pi$

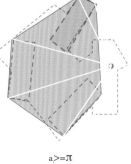

$a_j >= \pi$

Taro Narahara

Surfacing Stone: Digital Explorations in Masonry Curtain Wall Design

Martin Bechthold, Wes McGee, Monica Ponce de Leon

Seminar, Spring 2008 Students: Heather Boesch, Mathieu Lemieux Blanchard, Jessica Lisagor, Trevor Patt, Damon Sidel. Sponsor: International Masonry Institute. Support: International Union of Bricklayers and Allied Craftworkers.

The course researched the potential of emerging manufacturing techniques in the field of architecture to impact the use of a well-established material: masonry. Students collaborated with instructors in the design, fabrication, and assembly of a fragment of a curtain wall system that explored the use of stone as a building skin as impacted by the availability of digitally guided fabrication tools.

Historically the practice of architecture has been charged with negotiating the relationship between construction technique (tectonics) and the particular image of the building (aesthetics). Today, architects are in charge of "design," while the contractor is accountable for the "means of construction." But there has often been a very tenuous line between this delineation of responsibilities. Architects produce drawings with notes that suggest the means of construction, while the contractor generates shop drawings based on the architect's designs, and the architect "redlines" these drawings to insure that the original "intent" is carried out. This division has thus been an artificial one hiding the fact that architects have always designed with specific "means" in mind. The advent of digital manufacturing has introduced a twist in the legal distinction between "design intent" and "means of construction" through the elimination of the shop drawing process. With these methods the designer, not the builder, becomes responsible for the creation of drawings (now digital) that guide the manufacture of components for the assembly of buildings. Digital manufacturing technology is a shift away from knowledge-based construction methods, limited to the traditional forms of construction available in a particular locale; similarly, it represents a substantial change from conventional methods of mass production where repetition was the basis of economy. With computer-aided manufacturing (CAM), variation and customization no longer require an increase in costs due to specialized labor, exceptional manufacturing techniques, or extra setup charges.

The workshop focused on the use of robotically controlled abrasive waterjet cutting to research new possibilities for the design of buildings. Central to the investigation was the relationship between fabrication technique, material, geometry, and assembly. Performance areas such as substructure design, thermal factors, and acoustics were discussed along with the design of component anchors and connectors. Students modeled, prototyped, and constructed a series of mockups as preliminary studies for the final project, in which students collaborated with the instructors to create a rigorously developed curtain wall system, a fragment of which will be erected at full scale.

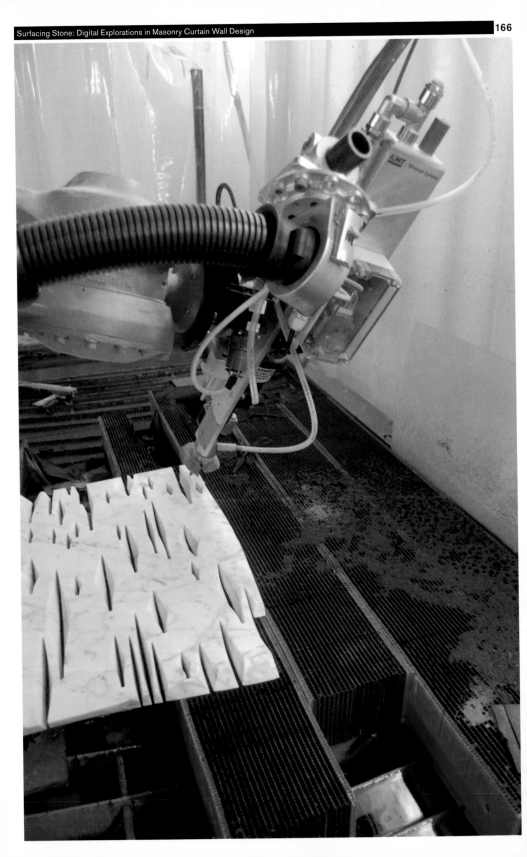

Mathieu Lemieux Blanchard

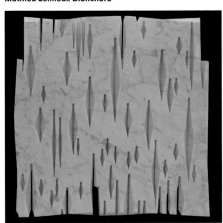 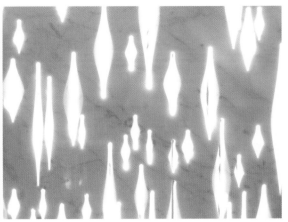

Heather Boesch

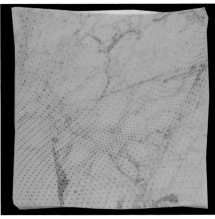 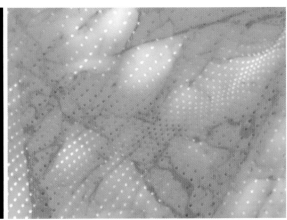

Jessica Lisagor

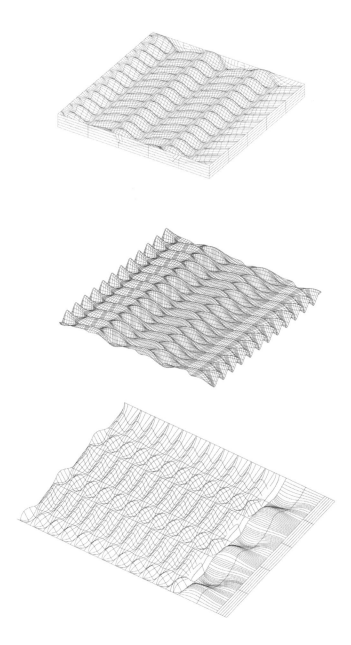

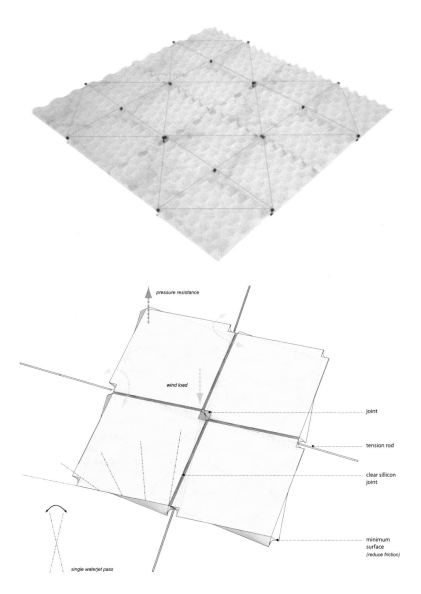

pressure resistance

wind load

joint

tension rod

clear sillicon
joint

minimum
surface
(reduce friction)

single waterjet pass

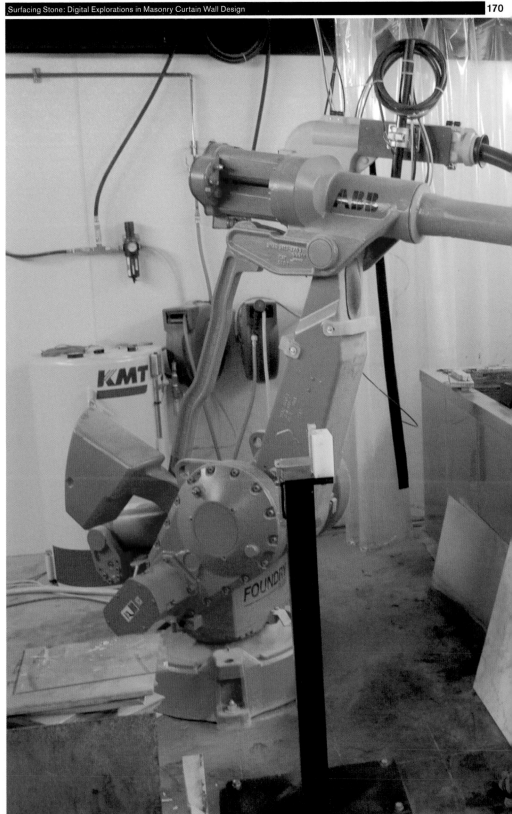

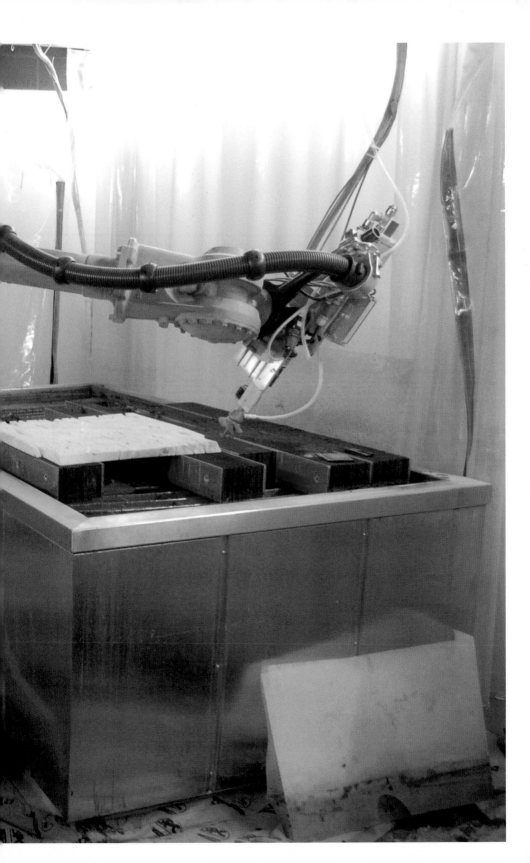

Responsive Skin

Michael Harris, David Jaubert; Toshiko Mori, advisor
Independent Study, Fall 2007

Responsive Skin was an experiment in the conception of generative processes as a viable means towards producing responsive and adaptive physical systems. The project was concerned with performative variability and its relevance to architectural form. It questioned the repetitive, isostatic nature of the architectural façade and explored a system that can vary based on a given set of architectural criteria.

The project proposed a system of unit-based aggregation in which the part-to-whole relationship is given by the ability of the unit to possess unique variation while remaining cohesive within the larger aggregation. The flatness of the architectural façade was questioned through the use of layered systems in which the threshold of the membrane is increased to a condition of interstitial depth, rather than graphic two-dimensionality. The layered system introduced the possibility of the façade to engender compound effects, enabling a more complex response to given architectural criteria.

The responsive skin was conceived as a flexible system that could be quickly and easily modified for experimentation. Written in Maya Embedded Language (MEL), all major properties of the system are modifiable through a graphical user interface which allows for a robust workflow in which each experiment can be refined through iterative versioning. The system was created exclusively through MEL using a process that can be divided primarily in two parts: the initial creation of geometry and the transformation of that geometry.

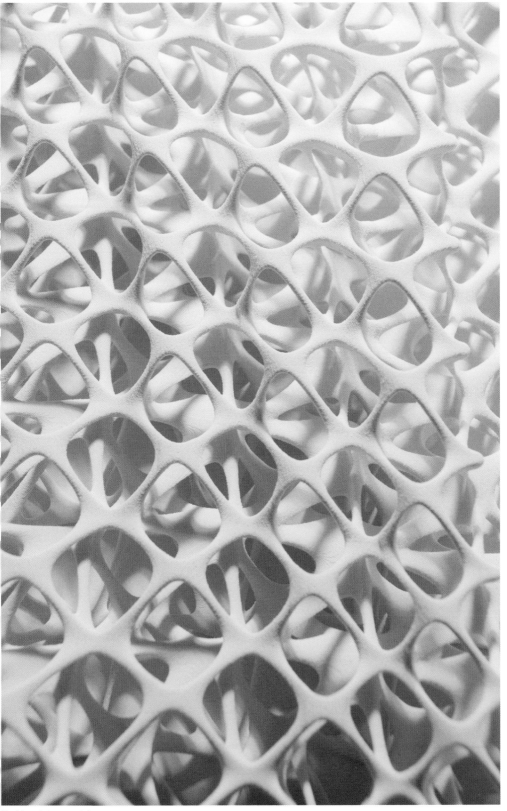

Rapid prototype model

Stack City
Behrang Behin
Thesis, Spring 2008

Stack City explores the architectural and urbanistic logic of the "carbon-neutral" or energy-efficient city, in the context of the development model that has emerged in the United Arab Emirates and is increasingly exported throughout the world. Specifically, it engages the phenomenon of new cities in the Gulf and their rationalization as self-contained totalities whose performance (be it in terms of real-estate value, economic sector development, or environmental impact) is "engineered" through master planning and design. While the urban models emerging in the Gulf may be problematic for their economic and technological determinism, they represent an increasingly prominent reality backed by an unprecedented investment of resources, and constitute a legitimate phenomenon that deserves attention. The thesis operates from within this new paradigm to develop a framework which, by taking the current urban models to their logical conclusion, also creates new possibilities for ways of life and architectural space.

While the master-planned new cities of the Gulf region provide an opportunity to go beyond the reproduction of existing models and imagine new forms of urbanism, commercially-driven developments have, for the most part, not exploited this opportunity in a meaningful way. Rather than confronting the peculiar qualities of an emerging urbanism by inventing an appropriate architectural expression, "newness" is either hidden behind references to existing and historical models, or superficially translated into the exuberant iconography that has become associated with the region.

With the Gulf as its context, Stack City is an investigation of the role of technology in shaping urban form and human experience in the energy-neutral city. In order to instigate a relationship between urban-scale infrastructural systems and spaces of inhabitation, a stack-effect solar-updraft system was adopted as an urban framework. This framework was chosen precisely because it imposes rigid technical constraints on the urban fabric, and therefore brings to the forefront the machinistic nature of the city, while it encourages the creation of a new form of urbanism which exists within this condition, but perhaps resists or disrupts the purity of its technologically deterministic logic.

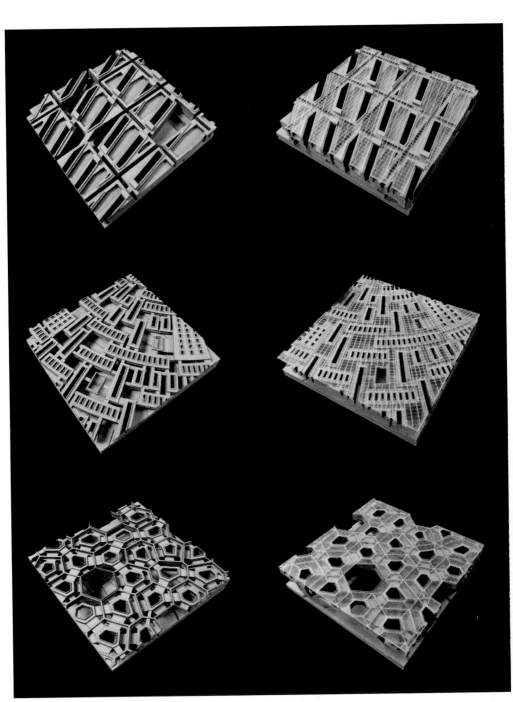

Mat studies

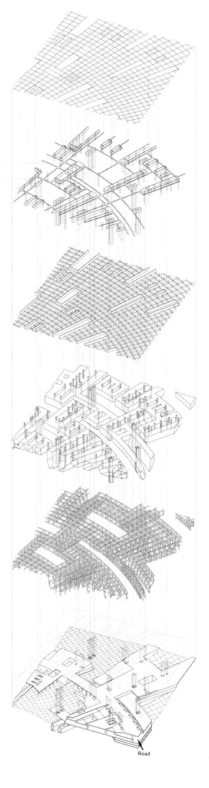

Glazed Canopy

Personal Rapid
Transit Network

Lobby

Private vehicle

Mechanical Systems
· Upper layer: Energy Infrastructures
· Lower layer: General Infrastructure
· Ventilation valves

Infill
· Mixed-Use
· Housing
· Office space

Private elevators

Communal elevators

Concrete Structural Framework

Ground
· Pedestrian Surface
· Limited auto routes and parking
· Communal and small-scale commercial program
  above ground
· Large-scale commercial, parking, communal facilities
  below ground

Parking

Road

Urban Stack components

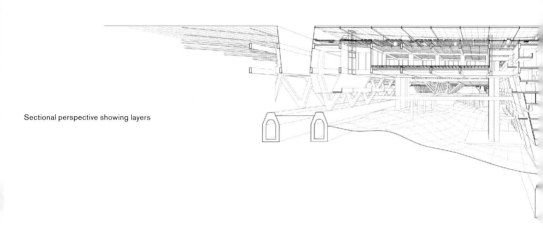

Sectional perspective showing layers

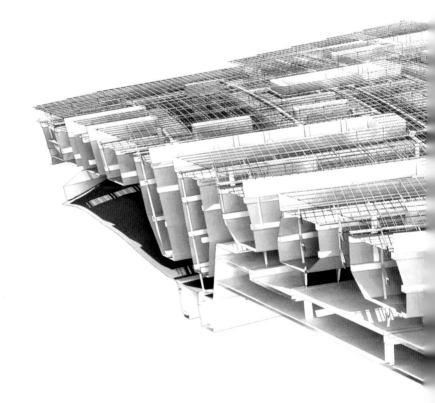

Urban Stack

Somerville High School

1 Emily Bonifaci   **2** Eamonn Hutton

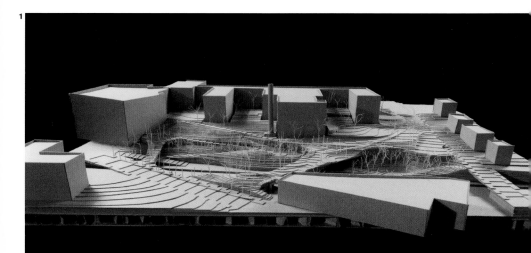

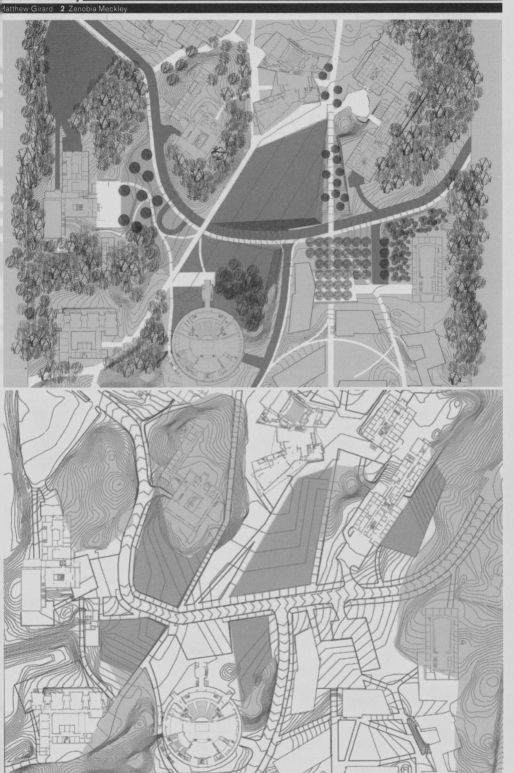

Core III Landscape Architecture, Fall 2007
West Concord
1 Leena Cho, Katie Powell, Maki Shindo **2** Danielle Meyer, Cynthia Silvey

1

Vegetation Strategy

Characteristics

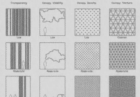

Deciduous Overstory

Deciduous & Evergreen Understory

Herbaceous Understory

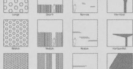

Constructed Wetland

Phytoremediation

Organizations

Groundcover

Sectional Shifts

Wildflower

Wallcover

Combination of Characters

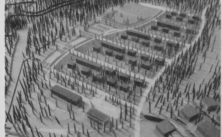

WEST CONCORD SITE PLAN   1:1000   CYNTHIA SILVEY, JULIE KIM, DANIELLE MEYER   GSD 1211

0   50   100   200   300   400
METERS

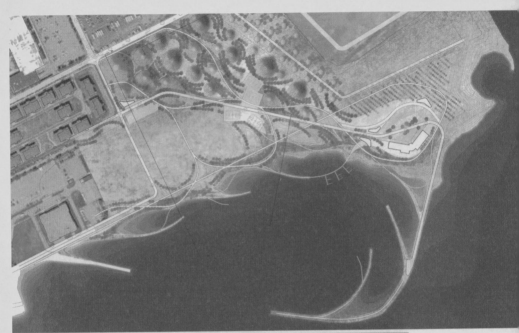

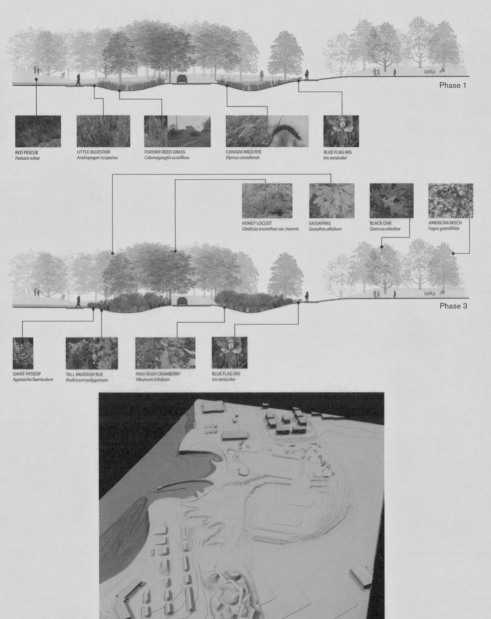

Phase 1

RED FESCUE
Festuca rubra

LITTLE BLUESTEM
Andropogon scoparius

FEATHER REED GRASS
Calamagrostis acutiflora

CANADA WILD RYE
Elymus canadensis

BLUE FLAG IRIS
Iris versicolor

HONEY LOCUST
Gleditsia tricanthos var. inermis

SASSAFRAS
Sassafras albidum

BLACK OAK
Quercus velutina

AMERICAN BEECH
Fagus grandifolia

Phase 3

GIANT HYSSOP
Agastache foeniculum

TALL MEADOW RUE
thalictrum polygamum

HIGH BUSH CRANBERRY
Viburnum trilobum

BLUE FLAG IRIS
Iris versicolor

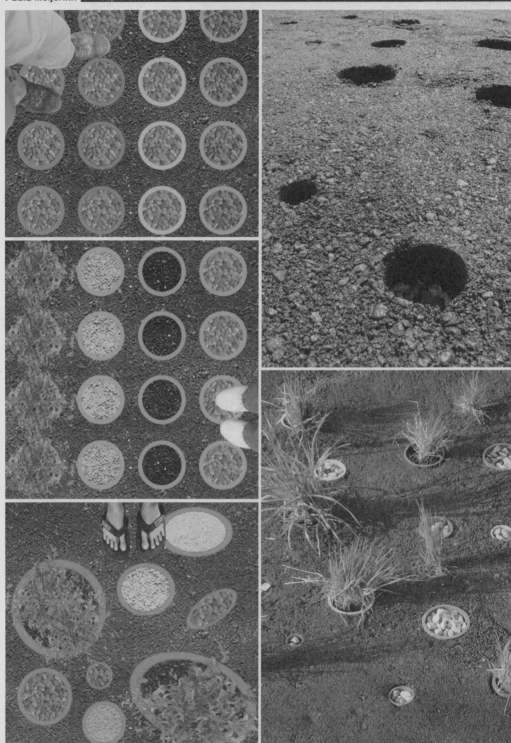

PVC Permeable Pavement pattern studies

Full scale mockup of PVC Permeable Pavement

Material

Excerpt: Systems for Inclusion
Shigeru Ban
Lecture, April 4, 2008

There have been too many natural disasters happening all over the world. But these are no longer natural disasters: they are man-made disasters. Earthquakes don't kill people; the collapse of buildings kills people. This is the responsibility of architects. Floods are also increasingly worse and more frequent because of deforestation, something architects are also indirectly responsible for, because we use a lot of timber for building. So this deforestation is also a part of our responsibility. Then, after these natural disasters, people lose their houses, and we need to build temporary houses, and we have to rebuild the villages and towns afterward. This is also the responsibility of architects. But we don't see too many architects in this kind of field.

Historically, architects have worked for privileged people. We have built religious temples and many other wonderful buildings; even now we work for corporations and developers, to visualize their power and their money through architecture. Making a monument is not really a bad thing; it is an important role of architects. But I think we also have another role, to use our knowledge and experience for the general public and for people in the minority.

After I graduated from Cooper Union, without any working experience, I started designing exhibitions. The first exhibition I designed was on Alvar Aalto, in 1986. Aalto was one of my favorite architects—I had been to Finland many times—and I wanted to design an exhibition like his architecture, but I didn't have the budget to use wood like Aalto did. I also didn't want to waste a precious material like wood for a temporary use, because after the exhibition the show would be dismantled. When I looked for an inexpensive material to replace the wood, I found the paper tube. It was all over my studio. We used trace paper and fax paper rolls; after the paper was gone, the old paper tubes remained, and I hated to throw them away. I knew that the tubes were very inexpensive, and that we could use different diameters and lengths in the exhibition. We used the small diameter like in Alvar Aalto's Viipuri Library, and the larger diameter was used for freestanding partitions. Though this was the first time I had used paper tubes, the material was much stronger than I expected. So I started testing it to use as a building material.

Paper, Wood and Bamboo: Shigeru Ban, GSD exhibition, 2003

I built my first paper tube structure in 1990. At the time, nobody was talking about recycling, ecology, or sustainable architecture. I used paper tubes because they were cheaper, and I was interested in using a raw material for the structure. The strength and durability of a building has nothing to do with the strength of the material: a concrete building can be destroyed easily by an earthquake, but this kind of lightweight paper tube structure cannot be. At the time I did not have a government permission to use this unusual material for building structures, so I had to have steel columns to support the roof. The paper tubes were just used as the walls for a single wing; there are 330 tubes in the space, each about 20 inches in diameter. There are also bigger tubes, about 4 feet in diameter, inside of which are the toilets.

In 1991 I designed a library addition for a poet, which the client was very kind to build as an experiment without getting the building permissions for the tubes. After seventeen years, it's still in very good condition. The addition uses four-inch diameter tubes with wooden connections. This time I used a post-tensioned structure, with steel cables inside of tubes, using the tension to connect the paper tubes within the joint without screws.

In 2000, I received the commission to design the Japanese pavilion for the Hannover Expo. The main theme of the Expo was environmental issues, so I was asked to use recycled material. But my interest was not when building was completed, but when it was demolished. The problem of Expo buildings is an environmental one: we create temporary buildings for half a year and then dismantle them, which creates a lot of industrial waste after the Expo ends. I wanted to use recycled material, but also I wanted to recycle the material I used after the building was demolished. So I worked with a local paper tube company to make sure the paper tube could be reused afterward. The structure used a vertical scaffolding, called props, which could be rotated by hand to push it up little by little, to create a three-dimensional curvature without depending on heavy cranes. I didn't want to use a concrete foundation, because concrete is a difficult material to recycle; instead, I designed a wooden box filled with sand, which became the main foundation of the building. I also didn't want to use a PVC membrane for the weather barrier, because it's not good for the environment, so I created a paper membrane that was highly protective and durable enough to meet German regulations. (As for the durability of paper tubes, waterproofing them is actually very easy. Water flowing on paper is not a problem: we usually drink orange juice from paper cartons. Paper is an industrial material, so waterproofing and fireproofing it is much actually easier than wood. The paper tubes we use are called Sonotubes, which are usually used for building construction as formwork for concrete columns. They are waterproof, and quite strong inside and outside; we are used to putting wet concrete inside them and exposing them on the outside, so they are already waterproof.)

I should say that this is not a pure paper tube structure. We had to make many compromises before we started construction, not because of German regulations but because of German authorities. We had tested it and done calculations to prove that the structure would meet the regulations, but the building administration office still didn't want to build any structure that they had never seen. So one of the biggest compromises we made was to introduce a timber arch. We collaborated with Frei Otto, and it was Otto's idea to design the first bridge structure out of paper tubes. The timber bridge makes the paper tubes stiff by triangulating the structure; the ladder-like arch can also be used for construction and maintenance. The building office then forced us to make the dimension of the timber four times bigger than necessary. So what used to be just a frame to enhance stiffness became a wooden arch structure, and the building became a hybrid structure of paper tubes and wood.

The joint is a very simple tape with a buckle. During erection, the paper tubes rotate three-dimensionally as they are lifted, and this simple joint allows this complicated movement of the paper tube. The end wall is made of paper honeycomb, to create a triangular structure. To be able to use the paper honeycomb, I first designed a small gallery for disabled children, using the paper honeycomb as the main roof structure; I tested it and got government permission, then applied it further in the Expo pavilion.

 I began working on disaster relief projects in Rwanda, in 1994. I was shocked to see people freezing with blankets; I had thought that most African countries were warm, but I found out that in Rwanda there is a very heavy rainy season. Because the shelters given by the United Nations were so poor, the people couldn't keep themselves warm without the blanket. I thought we have to improve their shelter; otherwise medical care wouldn't help them. So I went to the U.N. High Commissioner for Refugees in Geneva to propose reusing paper tubes as a building material.

In a typical shelter in that area, refugees have to cut down trees to make a frame for the plastic sheet given by the U.N. But over 2 million people became refugees in Rwanda, and they cut down all the trees. Where there used to be forest, there has been very severe deforestation and environmental problems. As these refugees went even farther to cut down more trees, the United Nations began providing them aluminum pipes instead, but they sold them for money—aluminum is a very expensive material in Africa—and they started cutting trees again. This is why the U.N. accepted my proposal to use the paper tube as a building material. I was also very lucky to get support from Vitra, one of the most important furniture companies in Europe. I went there to put up fifty units of the paper tube shelter in the monitoring stage, to find out whether the system is easy enough for the refugees to assemble by themselves, and also to test for termite problems, since there are many termites in Rwanda.

In 1995, over 5,600 people were killed in the earthquake in Kobe, Japan, and in the fire after the earthquake. Soon after, I met the Vietnamese population there, who were living in temporary houses made of plastic sheets in the park. It was a very unhealthy situation: on rainy days the inside got completely wet, and on sunny days the inside became so hot that it was impossible to stay inside. The neighbors also tried to kick them out, because they worried the park was becoming a slum. So we had to make the housing healthier, but also prettier, to be accepted by neighbors so they could keep living here. Even after the government started building temporary houses, these were all built outside of the city; most of the Vietnamese had their job in a particular part of the city, working for a particular factory, so if they had to move outside of the city, they would lose their jobs. This is why, even in such an unhealthy situation, they wanted to keep living in this park. So I started building temporary shelters with students made with paper tubes and plastic beer containers. (In Japan there are two major beer companies, Kirin and Asahi; I asked Kirin in particular to donate their plastic beer containers, because Asahi makes the plastic containers red, which doesn't go with the color of the paper tube.) The houses were all built by students during the summer, using plastic beer containers filled with sand for the foundation, with a double layer of membrane for natural ventilation.

I also went to the Catholic church in Kobe, because I knew many of the Vietnamese refugees went there. I asked the priest to rebuild the church out of paper tubes, but he didn't believe me in making a building out of paper. I commuted to the church every Sunday from Tokyo, and little by little, the priest was convinced; we could start this project, he said, as long as we did all the fundraising by ourselves, and if the building structure was built by volunteers. So we started fundraising.

The priest also said that he didn't want to have any icons or symbols of the Catholic church in the building, because he wanted to use it as a community space, not only as a church, inviting anyone from the neighborhood regardless of their religion. But I wanted to bring some of my experiences from churches all over the world. So I created a spatial gesture instead: a square exterior floor plan with an oval indoor space created by the paper tubes. The oval, of course, is brought from one of my favorite churches in Rome, designed by Bernini.

Everything was built by students. The paper church was there until two years ago, when the church decided to rebuild a permanent structure. The paper church was donated to an area in Taiwan where there had been a terrible earthquake in 1999, and where they asked us to donate; the whole building was dismantled, and now it is being rebuilt there, also by students.

So the building was in Kobe for twelve years; it became almost permanent—and now it actually is becoming permanent, because they are rebuilding it in Taiwan. Many of the buildings there were built in concrete, but have been totally destroyed by the earthquake. Even a building made of paper, then, can be permanent; as long as people love the structure, it can become the monument of the city. Architects love to make monuments for privileged people, but I was very happy to make a monument that was loved by people and became a permanent structure. I would like to keep building monuments for people.

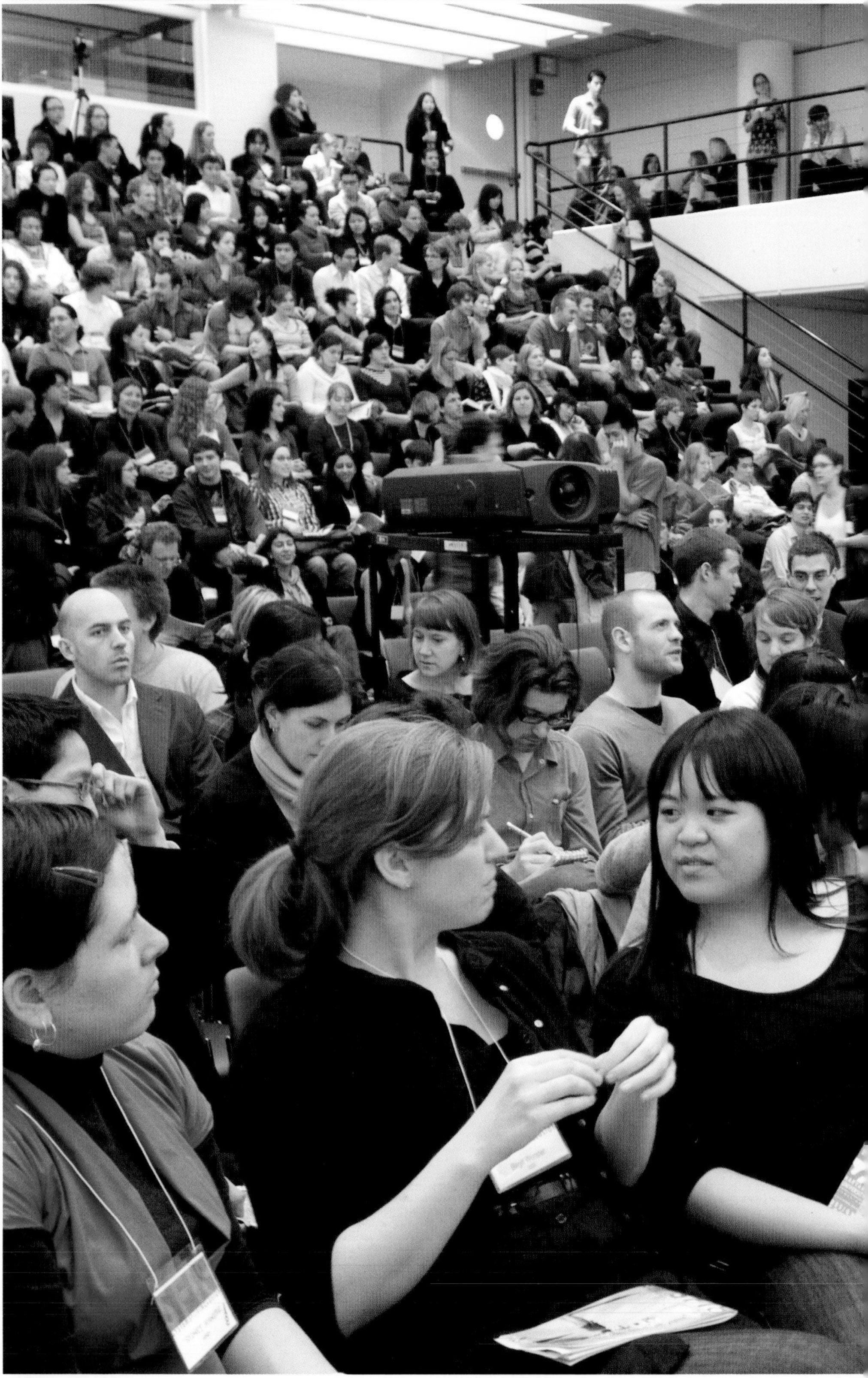

Soft Space: Agile Involution
Sustainable Strategies for Textile Architecture

Sheila Kennedy

Options Studio, Fall 2007 **Teaching Associate:** Tonya Ohnstad. **Students:** Michelle Chang, Ryan Culligan, Sabeen Hasan, Maciej Kaczynski, Sophia Lau, Jessica Lisagor, Mara Marcu, Douglas Miller, Cheyne Owens, Diane Rhyu, David Shanks, Lukas Thorn. **Sponsor:** Saint-Gobain.

The studio explored the integration of flexible solar nano-materials with lightweight textile construction as a new medium for soft space and distributed power generation. A set of intriguing formal problems is produced by the continuity and specificity required for the structural integrity of textile construction and the competing need for vertical disruptions in the textile surface necessary for the integration of flexible solar arrays.
Using digital modeling and pattern-making techniques for textile construction, students explored the soft space surface geometries of the agile involution, the exceptional condition (present in forms such as the torus, the klein bottle, and the heliocoid) when a surface turns in on itself, moving smoothly from horizontal to vertical curvatures as its spatial reading transforms from volume to void.

Using a lightweight textile construction, students designed projects for a Public Market Hall and Bus Terminal Building in the Centro District of Zacatecas, Mexico. The Centro District is an important urban intersection which connects different economic neighborhoods with major Mexican cities and remote villages in the Sierra Madre. The studio took a non-nostalgic approach to the municipal needs of the program and the fluid demands of small-scale market vendors in the economies of the informal sector. Students engaged efficient textile spanning geometries with formal strategies of involution to create passages for daylighting, ventilation, and circulation, and to provide public resources for renewable distributed power to drive solid state lighting, fans for ventilation, and water purification through exposure to ultraviolet radiation.

Excellent solar latitudes, a vibrant mix of public needs, and an extraordinary topographical history of urban infrastructure in mining tunnels, cable cars, ramped streets, and stairway passages provide the urban context for the next generation of fabric infrastructure. Students were encouraged to develop their own understanding of the material and spatial properties of sustainable textile architecture and to combine and/or decouple the known categories and behaviors of urban infrastructure, object appliance "fixture," and architectural structure and surface as produced by 20th-century centralized distribution paradigms.

Students visited the production facility of Saint-Gobain, the studio sponsor and a leading global manufacturer of high-performance architectural membranes, to learn about the material properties of these membranes and their computerized manufacturing, cutting, patterning, and fabrication processes. Students worked in teams to analyze selected fabric structure precedents and explore how known fabric forms may be modified and morphed using 3D modeling software. The re-discovery of "lost" (pre-digital) techniques of modernism, drawn from the work of Frei Otto, Pier Luigi Nervi, and Felix Candela, enabled students to verify the digital form-making of their design projects with the physical modeling of complex fabric surfaces.

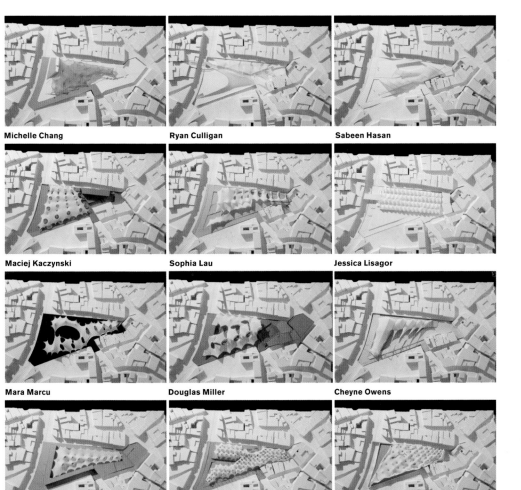

Michelle Chang

Ryan Culligan

Sabeen Hasan

Maciej Kaczynski

Sophia Lau

Jessica Lisagor

Mara Marcu

Douglas Miller

Cheyne Owens

Diane Rhyu

David Shanks

Lukas Thorn

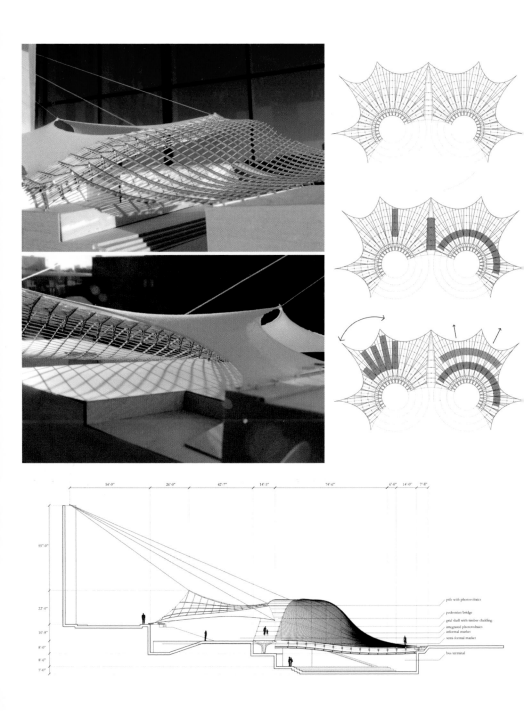

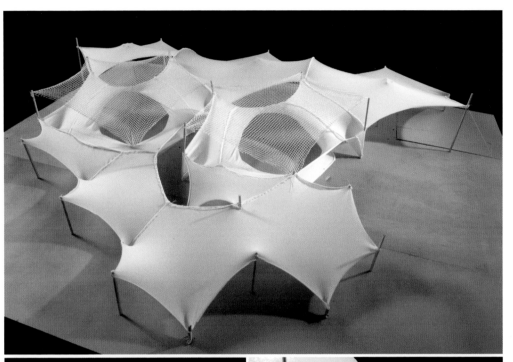

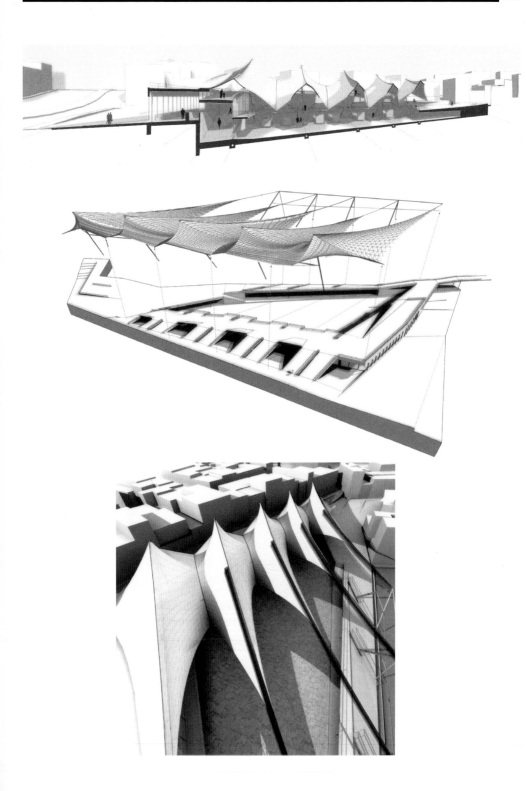

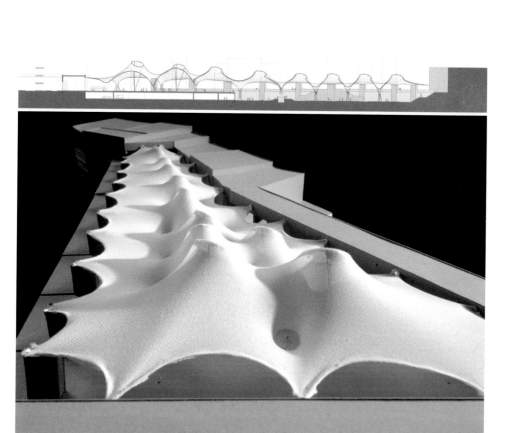

Materials Constructions Processes:
Building with Wood–Building with Steel

Jonathan Levi, Thomas Schroepfer
Seminar, Spring 2008

The course introduced a conceptual framework for the design of building assemblies, as informed by a clear understanding of construction technologies and the properties of building materials. Building materials were presented and analyzed with emphasis on their physical and architectural properties, functions, and behavior in manufactured and installed assemblies. The designs of building envelopes in various materials were examined as integrated subsystems of components in relation to the forces that shape their composition. The methodology and format of the design of building detailing were discussed, and the roles of the various participants in this process were reviewed.

The course was conducted in two modules: Building with Wood, with Jonathan Levi, and Building with Steel, with Thomas Schroepfer.

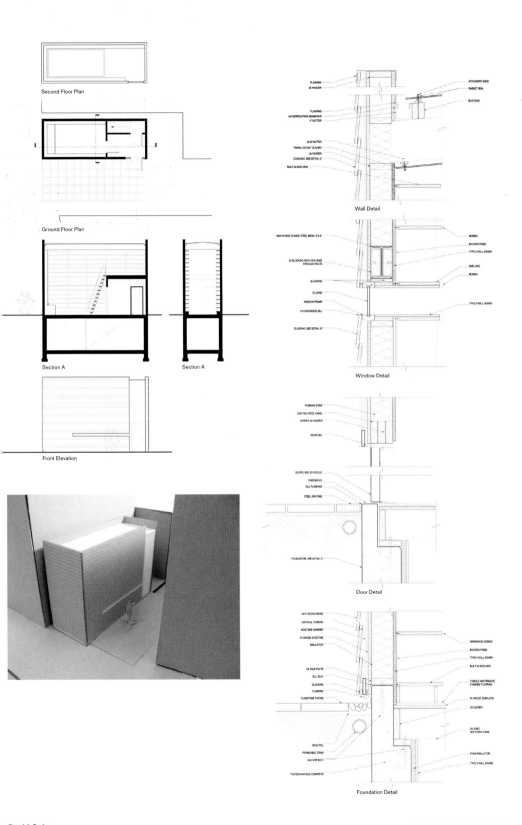

Second Floor Plan

Ground Floor Plan

Section A

Section A

Front Elevation

Wall Detail

Window Detail

Door Detail

Foundation Detail

David Gale

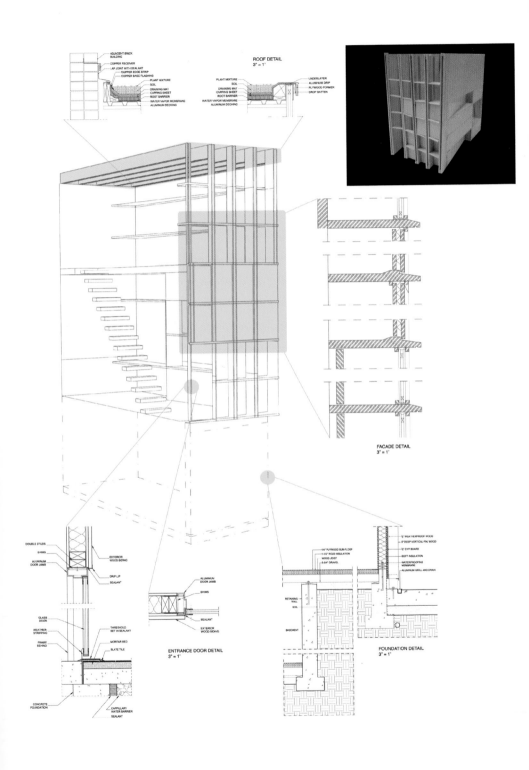

ROOF DETAIL
3" = 1'

FACADE DETAIL
3" = 1'

ENTRANCE DOOR DETAIL
3" = 1'

FOUNDATION DETAIL
3" = 1'

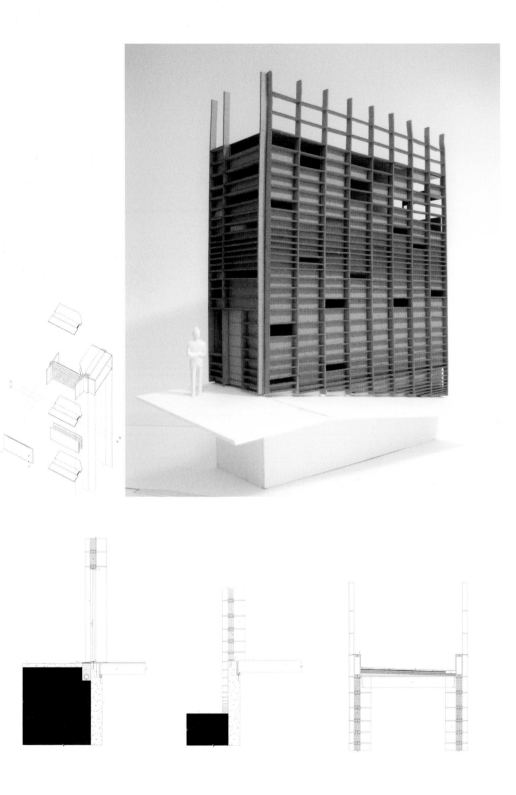

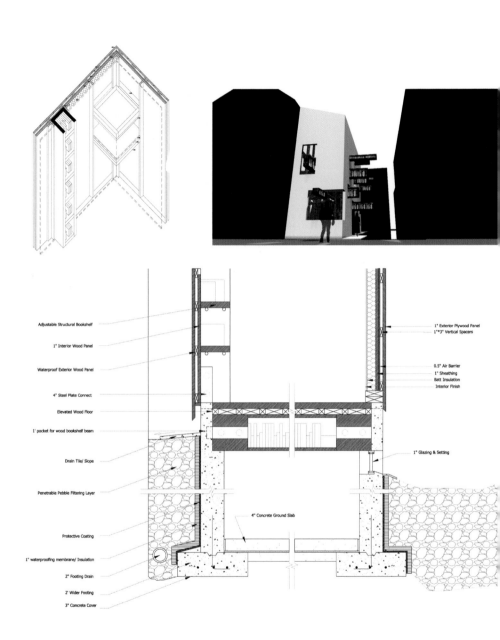

Adjustable Structural Bookshelf

1" Interior Wood Panel

Waterproof Exterior Wood Panel

4" Steel Plate Connect

Elevated Wood Floor

1' pocket for wood bookshelf beam

Drain Tile/ Slope

Penetrable Pebble Filtering Layer

Protective Coating

1" waterproofing membrane/ Insulation

2" Footing Drain

2' Wider Footing

3" Concrete Cover

1" Exterior Plywood Panel
1"*3" Vertical Spacers

0.5" Air Barrier
1" Sheathing
Batt Insulation
Interior Finish

1" Glazing & Setting

4" Concrete Ground Slab

Wei-Nien Chen

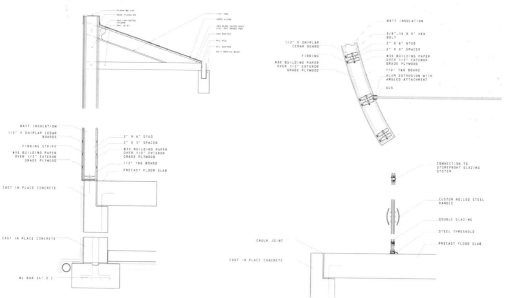

BATT INSULATION

1/2" V SHIPLAP CEDAR BOARD

FIRRING

#30 BUILDING PAPER OVER 1/2" EXTERIOR GRADE PLYWOOD

3/8"-16 X 5" HEX BOLT

2" X 4" STUD

2" X 3" SPACER

#30 BUILDING PAPER OVER 1/2" EXTERIOR GRADE PLYWOOD

1/2" T&G BOARD

ALUM EXTRUSION WITH ANGLED ATTACHMENT

GLS

BATT INSULATION

1/2" V SHIPLAP CEDAR BOARDS

FIRRING STRIPS

#30 BUILDING PAPER OVER 1/2" EXTERIOR GRADE PLYWOOD

CAST IN PLACE CONCRETE

CAST IN PLACE CONCRETE

#4 BAR 24" O.C.

2" X 6" STUD

2" X 3" SPACER

#30 BUILDING PAPER OVER 1/2" EXTERIOR GRADE PLYWOOD

1/2" T&G BOARD

PRECAST FLOOR SLAB

CONNECTION TO STOREFRONT GLAZING SYSTEM

CUSTOM ROLLED STEEL HANDLE

DOUBLE GLAZING

STEEL THRESHOLD

PRECAST FLOOR SLAB

CAULK JOINT

CAST IN PLACE CONCRETE

Eli Allen

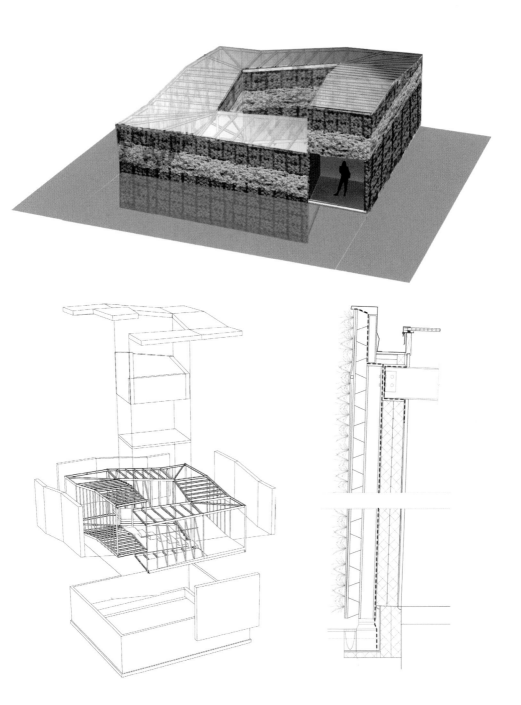

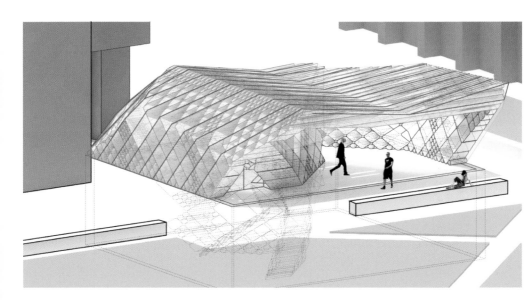

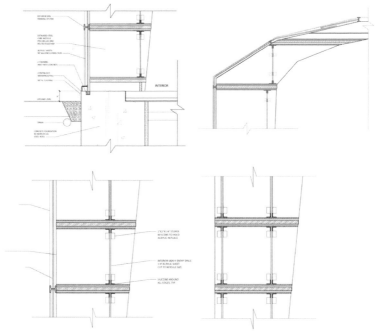

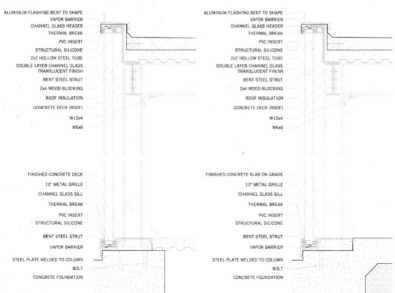

ALUMINUM FLASHING BENT TO SHAPE
VAPOR BARRIER
CHANNEL GLASS HEADER
THERMAL BREAK
PVC INSERT
STRUCTURAL SILICONE
2x2 HOLLOW STEEL TUBE
DOUBLE LAYER CHANNEL GLASS
TRANSLUCENT FINISH
BENT STEEL STRUT
2x4 WOOD BLOCKING
ROOF INSULATION
CONCRETE DECK (ROOF)

W10x4
W6x6

ALUMINUM FLASHING BENT TO SHAPE
VAPOR BARRIER
CHANNEL GLASS HEADER
THERMAL BREAK
PVC INSERT
STRUCTURAL SILICONE
2x2 HOLLOW STEEL TUBE
DOUBLE LAYER CHANNEL GLASS
TRANSLUCENT FINISH
BENT STEEL STRUT
2x4 WOOD BLOCKING
ROOF INSULATION
CONCRETE DECK (ROOF)

W10x4
W6x6

FINISHED CONCRETE DECK
12" METAL GRILLE
CHANNEL GLASS SILL
THERMAL BREAK
PVC INSERT
STRUCTURAL SILICONE

BENT STEEL STRUT
VAPOR BARRIER
STEEL PLATE WELDED TO COLUMN
BOLT
CONCRETE FOUNDATION

FINISHED CONCRETE SLAB ON GRADE
12" METAL GRILLE
CHANNEL GLASS SILL
THERMAL BREAK
PVC INSERT
STRUCTURAL SILICONE

BENT STEEL STRUT
VAPOR BARRIER
STEEL PLATE WELDED TO COLUMN
BOLT
CONCRETE FOUNDATION

Justin Chen

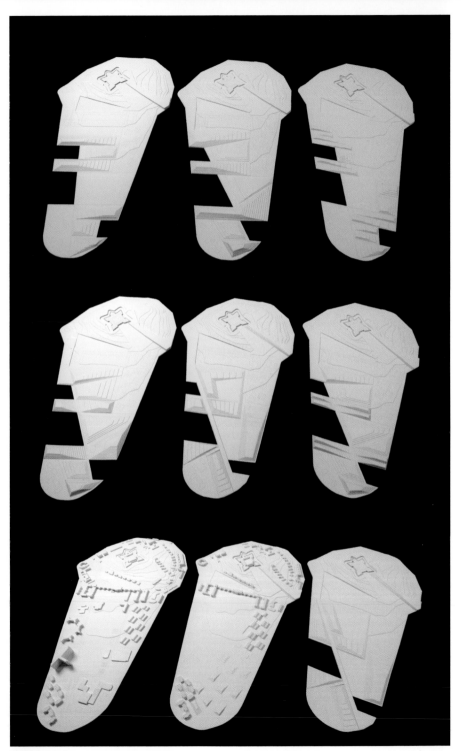

Masterplan studies

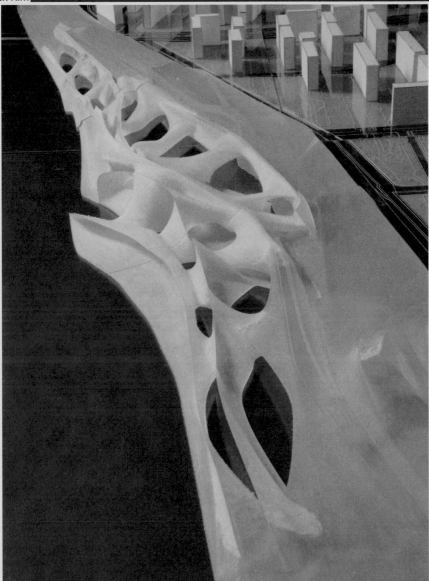

Model of park at river/city edge

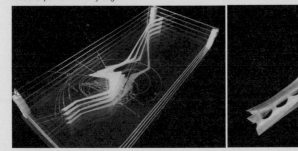

Study models

GSD Public Lecture series posters

HARVARD GSD FALL 2007

GSD LECTURES

AUG 22–OCT 3 ECOLOGY.DESIGN.SYNERGY

SEPT 17 ECOLOGY.DESIGN.SYNERGY
EXHIBITION OPENING LECTURE FOR ECOLOGY.DESIGN.SYNERGY WITH MATTHIAS SCHULER, TRANSSOLAR CLIMATE ENGINEERING, STUTTGART

DEPARTMENT LECTURES

SEPT 18 ANGELO BUCCI
PRINCIPAL, SPBR ARQUITECTOS, SÃO PAULO; VISITING DESIGN CRITIC, GSD; RECENT PROJECTS BY SPBR ARQUITECTOS

SEPT 19 RYUE NISHIZAWA
RYUE NISHIZAWA, RECENT PROJECTS

SEPT 25 LIAT MARGOLIS AND ALEXANDER ROBINSON
LIAT MARGOLIS, INSTRUCTOR, GSD MATERIALS ECOLOGIES AND LANDSCAPE ARCHITECTS, SUBSTRATES
ALEXANDER ROBINSON, LANDSCAPE ARCHITECT, LOS ANGELES STATES — INNOVATIVE MATERIALS AND TECHNOLOGIES

SEPT 26 HANI RASHID
PRINCIPAL, ASYMPTOTE ARCHITECTURE, NEW YORK; ASYMPTOTE 3.0

OCT 1 OSCAR NIEMEYER 100:
JOAQUIM GUEDES AND JOSÉ PASQUAL

OCT 2 FARES EL-DAHDAH
ASSOCIATE PROFESSOR OF ARCHITECTURE, RICE UNIVERSITY; ETERNAL HOUSE AT 4 PM; THE MAKING OF BRASÍLIA

OCT 9 KENNETH FRAMPTON
WARE PROFESSOR OF ARCHITECTURE, COLUMBIA UNIVERSITY; ARCHITECTURE IN THE AGE OF GLOBALIZATION

OCT 10 TRIBUTE TO WILLIAM LEMESSURIER
CELEBRATION OF HIS TEACHING AND WORK

OCT 15 JEPPE AAGAARD ANDERSEN

OCT 16 BRENDAN MACFARLANE
PRINCIPAL, JACOB + MACFARLANE, PARIS; RECENT WORK

OCT 17 ERWAN BOUROULLEC
DESIGNER, RONAN ET ERWAN BOUROULLEC, PARIS — RONAN AND ERWAN BOUROULLEC

OCT 17–NOV 14 STUDIO WORKS FALL 06–SPRING 07

OCT 24 CARL STEINITZ
ALEXANDER AND VICTORIA WILEY RESEARCH PROFESSOR OF LANDSCAPE ARCHITECTURE AND PLANNING, GSD—
FREDERICK LAW OLMSTED LECTURE / LANDSCAPE PLANNING: A HISTORY OF INFLUENTIAL IDEAS

OCT 30 GEORGE L. LEGENDRE
ARCHITECT AND EDUCATOR, IJP CORPORATION AND ARCHITECTURAL ASSOCIATION, LONDON — NEK THINGS

NOV 6 EVA JIRICNA
ARCHITECT, EVA JIRICNA ARCHITECTS, LONDON — SELECTED WORK

NOV 7 CRAIG WEBB
PARTNER, GEHRY PARTNERS, LOS ANGELES — PROJECTS FOR URBANITY / LECTURE STARTS AT 6:30 PM

NOV 9 MK12
THE REAL REASON AND FRIENDS? DUGAN, MK12, KANSAS CITY / IMAGE

NOV 13 SARAH WHITING
ABTE YEAR / REFLECTIONS ON MY OWN PRACTICE / W.W. SYSTEM — WHW PRINCETON, NEW JERSEY + SUPER

NOV 14 WILLOUGHBY SHARP

NOV 19 ARATA ISOZAKI
ARCHITECT, ARATA ISOZAKI AND ASSOCIATES, TOKYO / KUI / THINK MAT

NOV 27 PHILIPPE RAHM
PRINCIPAL, PHILIPPE RAHM ARCHITECTES, PARIS – NO ONE LAB/DECOSTERD —
THE SHADOW OF THE ATMOSPHERIC UTILIZE THE PROJECTS BY PHILIPPE RAHM ARCHITECTES

NOV 28 FRANCISCO MANGADO
PRINCIPAL, MANGADO Y ASOCIADOS, S.L., PAMPLONA, SPAIN LEFT MANGO ARCHITECTURE

NOV 29–JAN 13 OLYMPIC SCULPTURE PARK, SEATTLE ART MUSEUM

DEC 4 DIALOGUE: JACQUES HERZOG AND PETER EISENMAN
JACQUES HERZOG, PRINCIPAL, HERZOG & DE MEURON, BASEL + PETER EISENMAN, PRINCIPAL, EISENMAN ARCHITECTS, NEW YORK

DEC 5 VERONICA RUDGE GREEN PRIZE: WEISS/MANFREDI
VERONICA RUDGE GREEN PRIZE IN URBAN DESIGN TO WEISS/MANFREDI ARCHITECTURE,
LANDSCAPE, URBANISM FOR OLYMPIC SCULPTURE PARK, SEATTLE ART MUSEUM

HARVARD UNIVERSITY GRADUATE SCHOOL OF DESIGN
PIPER AUDITORIUM, GUND HALL, 48 QUINCY STREET, CAMBRIDGE, MA 02138
SEE WWW.GSD.HARVARD.EDU/EVENTS FOR MORE INFORMATION
UNLESS NOTED OTHERWISE LECTURES START AT 6 PM AND ARE FREE AND
OPEN TO THE PUBLIC

HARVARD GSD SPRING 2008

EXHIBITIONS

JAN 28–MARCH 16 DIRTY WORK: TRANSFORMING LANDSCAPE IN THE NON-FORMAL CITY OF THE AMERICAS

GSD LECTURES

JAN 30 ROBERT NEUWIRTH

FEB 6 JANET MARIE SMITH

FEB 12 ALBERT POPE

FEB 20 WINKA DUBBELDAM

FEB 26 INÈS LAMUNIÈRE

FEB 27 WANG SHU

MARCH 4 TEDDY CRUZ

MARCH 5 DAVID HICKEY

MARCH 6 EDWARD GLAESER

MARCH 11 REGINE LEIBINGER

MARCH 12 IÑAKI ÁBALOS

MARCH 13 PROGRESS IN PROCESS

MARCH 18 RECONSTRUCTING DESIGN PRACTICE

MARCH 31–MAY 21 AGA KHAN AWARD FOR ARCHITECTURE THE TENTH AWARD CYCLE, 2005–2007

APRIL 1 VLADIMIR DJUROVIC

APRIL 2 HOMI BHABHA

APRIL 3 BLACK COMMUNITY: FUTUREPRESENT

APRIL 4 SHIGERU BAN

APRIL 4–6 SYSTEMS FOR INCLUSION 8

APRIL 8 LUIS FERNÁNDEZ-GALIANO

APRIL 9 TOSHIKO MORI

APRIL 11 PETER WALKER

APRIL 14 CHARLES WALDHEIM

APRIL 17–19 ART IN THE LIFE OF THE CITY

APRIL 22 MATTHEW GANDY

APRIL 23 NEW GEOGRAPHIES: DESIGN, AGENCY, TERRITORY

APRIL 25 BUCKMINSTER FULLER, IN EFFECT

APRIL 28 SANFORD KWINTER

APRIL 29 KENNETH FRAMPTON

APRIL 30 MIA LEHRER

JUNE 4–AUG 6 COMMENCEMENT EXHIBITION

HARVARD UNIVERSITY GRADUATE SCHOOL OF DESIGN
PIPER AUDITORIUM, GUND HALL, 48 QUINCY STREET, CAMBRIDGE, MA 02138
SEE WWW.GSD.HARVARD.EDU/EVENTS FOR MORE INFORMATION
LECTURES START AT 6 PM AND ARE FREE AND OPEN TO THE PUBLIC

Student Group Lectures 2007–2008

Student Group Lecture posters

View 2008

Harvard Design Magazine 27

Harvard Design Magazine 28

Studio Works 12

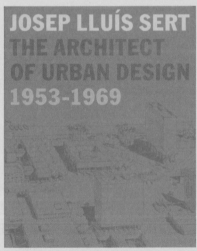

Josep Lluís Sert: The Architect of Urban Design,
1953–1969
Eric Mumford and Hashim Sarkis
Yale University Press / GSD

Olympic Sculpture Park for the Seattle Art Museum
Joan Busquets

The Function of Ornament
Farshid Moussavi
and Michael Kubo
Actar / GSD

Project Zagreb: Transition as Condition,
Strategy, Practice
Eve Blau and Ivan Rupnik
Actar / GSD

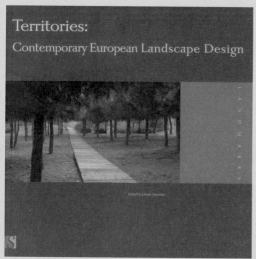

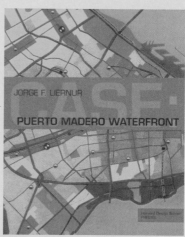

Territories: Contemporary European Landscape Design
Joseph Disponzio
Spacemaker Press / GSD

CASE: Puerto Madero Waterfront
Jorge Francisco Liernur
Prestel / GSD

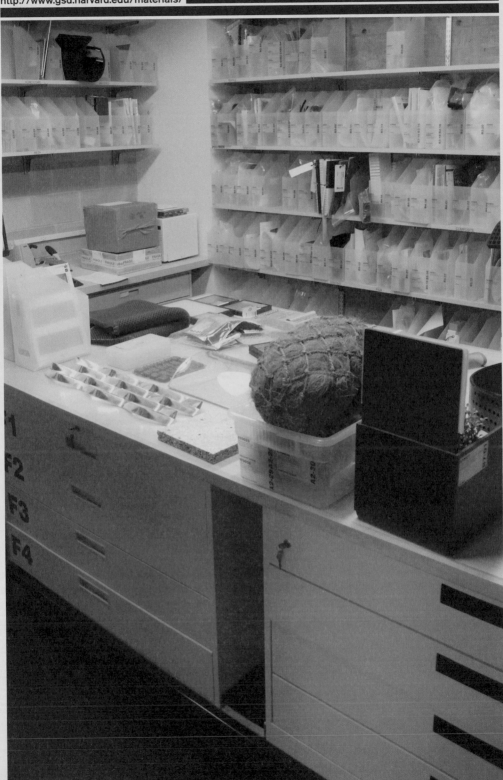

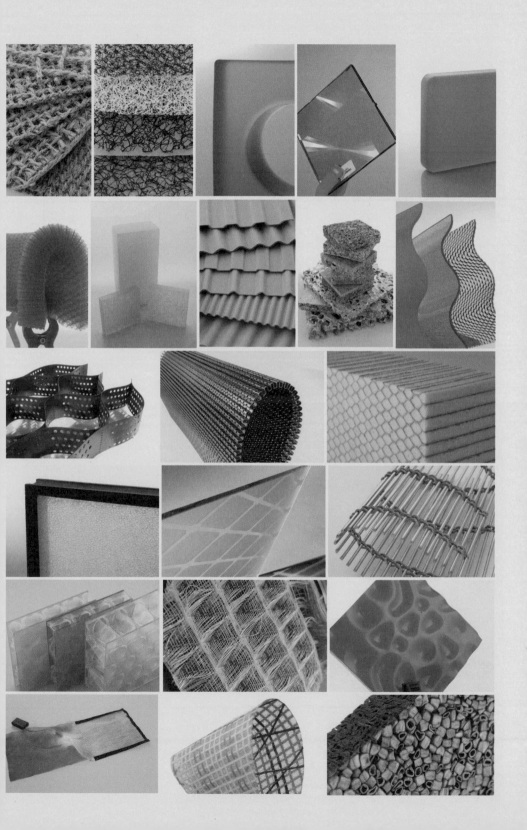

Discipline

Excerpt: Jacques Herzog and Peter Eisenman
Jeff Kipnis, moderator
Dialogue, December 4, 2007

Jeff Kipnis: These are two architects who have fought a life-long battle to rescue architecture from the banality and mediocrity which it can lapse into in a kind of professionalism. Both have made careers of challenging received wisdoms of what constitutes good buildings. Jacques, you have said a number of times that, however interesting post-humanism might be (whatever that might mean), Herzog and de Meuron are humanist architects. To me, this means that there is a primacy of the sensory pleasures of the building that you would take to be a given condition. I think Peter, on the other hand, believes that to cast suspicion on those pleasures and experiences of the building is the primary role of architecture, and to think about a building might be its primary cultural project. What do you mean by wanting to be the last humanist architect?

Jacques Herzog: We conceive of our architecture basically as an archaic thing, in the way that it appeals to all the senses of the human being. Being human means that we can perceive the world; we can perceive our own existence, not only with the brains but with all the five senses we have. It's clear that we live in a time where the visual has become more dominant than other senses. This has, of course, an impact on architecture and on other media and cultural phenomena. Architecture survives as long as we are able and willing to appeal to all these senses in a similar way and not give priority to one more than to another. In that sense, we see ourselves as in the tradition of humanism. Ultimately all architects are measured by this, whether or not they focus on it.

Harvard University
Graduate School of Design

JK: Peter, you seem uncomfortable with my characterization of your position. But you wouldn't say you produce a sensuous architecture?

Peter Eisenman: Jacques and I would agree when he says there's too much of the visual in the world. I do think his work, and especially some of the more recent work, is importantly visual, and I would also say that my late work in a funny way is also importantly visual, no matter how much both of us might agree that the visual is too dominant. The interesting question, I think, is the subtle difference between his use of the visual and my use of the visual.

JH: Our work was always very much about the visual. Everybody knows how we started our career, from the side of art rather than from the side of architecture. And, logically, all these issues of perception are theoretically much more strongly rooted in the world of art than in architecture. Even the very simple shapes and our early collaborations were very much perception-driven; our conceptions go back to pre-structuralist French philosophy. Which means that, ultimately, in the deep rooting, our work is more conceptual than phenomenological. It's conceptual because it's held together with thinking, with concepts of thinking. But the result is very sensual. Ultimately, once we reach a certain level, the visual is always transcended into other issues like the concept.

JK: Jacques has said that when you're in a building, if the building doesn't deliver its architecture to you there in and in that sense, it's the worst possible architecture. Peter, you would disagree. There's a reason, either political or cultural, that you want to remove the architectural connoisseur or the subject of your architecture from that experience. What would you say is the role of architecture in the world? If it turns out to be located in whether the building delivers its architectural proposition in the immediacy of the building or not, that's something that we should unfold.

PE: What good is reading a book for the story and then forgetting about it? The whole idea of reading a book is that it informs your environment; it informs how you live. There's nothing more boring than going into a dumb, spectacular building, saying, "Oh, this is great," and walking away. What you're supposed to do—with literature, with film, with architecture, with any art—is to go away and to have a thought about it, whether it's a sensual thought or a conceptual thought.

JH: I didn't say, "That's it." It's like art or anything you look at. Ultimately, always and only, exclusively, the thinking, the mental, the conceptual interests me. But you conceive it and then it becomes physical. Our buildings very often are seductive and beautiful, and I cannot deny that this was always something that attracted me in life. Being attracted and attractive is the ultimate thing: intellectually, physically, sensually. But, because we do buildings like that, many people believe—and this is the cliché—that what is beautiful is also stupid. So the buildings look good, have a façade, and that's it. They forget to look at the interior, the structure, or anything else.

PE: What is important is to try and define the difference in what kind of thinking you're talking about, because I think there's a difference when you go to one of your projects and when you go to one of mine. We ought to try and tease out that difference.

JK: Jacques, you publish your process; your office is generous in the sense that you let people know how you work. When the Prada Tokyo store was published, for example, you showed sixteen models of different material treatments of the shape. You showed a few sketches about the regulating lines of the building from which you got a shape—it's not a form—and then a set of experiments that you looked at, judged one successfully, and pursued that. But the built result of the work has no indication of the process whatsoever. In fact there is no built evidence of process in any of your work, although there is evidence of the process in your presentations. The Laban dance center is another example: to create the sense of freezing a balletic moment in the building, with both the interior and the exterior, means making sure that there is no trace of any process in the building itself. Everything Peter does is about making sure that the evidence and the residues of the process are in the building; the process is the justification of the building, much like it is in Abstract Expressionist work. Your work withholds that. Is this a clue into the different ambitions of the work?

JH: I'm much more interested in the process to get to the best result than to exposing the process in the finished building, because the finished building is there and I am somewhere else. When I am working on the building, I am very close. But as soon as it's finished, it needs to live without me.

JK: When you look at the Schaulager in Basel or at Laban, built in isolated places of no particular contextual interests, their pleasures are very erotic. They are essentially about urban production: art is an urban production, and you manage to make the outside of the Schaulager feel like the interior of a museum space; ballet is an urban production, and Laban floats. It's quite an extraordinary thing to take a set of experiences that belong to different place, make them real there, and ignore the context.

JH: The two buildings couldn't be more different because Laban is totally ephemeral, almost like a kind of a cloud. Schaulager, the other one, is extremely earthy. It's almost, as you said, the inside turned out.

PE: Jacques, I have a question for you. You would agree that your work is about ideas and the implementation of ideas. Yet, I can't understand, and you have to tell me, how it's possible in a large office, where you have to keep producing buildings, to have so many ideas. How can you work when you have so many things to do, so many clients to see? How is it possible to keep up the level of when you were smaller, more intense? I think it's a real issue for me, for you, for Frank Gehry, for Rem Koolhaas…

JH: There is no doubt that we have now probably reached the size where this is a real issue. We've reached a limit. We cannot grow more except if we change the way we work.

JK: You have 250 people at the office, 38 active projects, 6 team leaders, roughly.

JH: Yes. We have to increase the number of team leaders. I think that we are very well organized, but still we have reached the limit, there is no doubt. One thing is the architecture, the project; another thing is the project of your company, of your life, ultimately, of how you work and how you deal with clients. I do very little socializing. I don't see clients very often. I'm extremely focused on coaching the teams and working on the projects. But even then you cannot extend without a limit, and we are really very actively thinking what we do five years from now and ten years from now. Should the company continue? Should we sell something? Should we have more partners?

JK: I really think I could write a set of instructions on how to produce an Eisenman project. It would change because the office grows, but whenever there is a project, I can see how it comes out of the way Peter works. Every time Peter does a building, I know why. In Laban, however, the building has an intense capacity to reveal itself in the ways you have talked about; but it reveals nothing about how you work. There is nothing in your work

that reveals any of the ways that you produce an architectural insight.

JH: I think that's the ultimate result of conceptual work. If we were even slightly attached to certain tastes or a prioris, we couldn't do that.

PE: That's interesting because I think I am attached to a prioris. I give summer seminars in the office. We set up the discourse for the year and then everything falls into that discourse.

JK: Peter, you work critically: you will set up a process and set a few people working on it and then work as a critic. The process will get going and then you will review the work and criticize it towards its end. Jacques, I understand that you work in teams, but do you bring an idea to each project?

JH: We try to define the guidelines in a rolling kind of process. If you set up the rules from the very beginning, you will destroy everything. On the other hand, if you are too loose, you will also not get anywhere. So it's not so easy to say how we do it.

PE: But isn't it looking for accidents? The whole idea of setting up rules is looking for the accidents, the flaws, the errors and going with those, being willing to move. Our recent Abu Dhabi project actually came out of being on a thesis jury here at Harvard, taking the sandwich of three layers that the student had presented and saying, "Hey, he screwed it up—but I know how to work this." I was fascinated by the potential of section by putting these layers together; I saw it within a theoretical context of what I would call the partial figure. It was accidental. I saw something in what someone was doing that had nothing to do with what he was doing, and ran with it.

JK: How would you both individually translate your methods of architecture into pedagogy?

PE: The big change in pedagogy, I think, whether for good or for bad, is that the schools that I went to and was working against were set up to feed people into the profession. They were not set up to learn about the discipline. I think the relationship that existed, and still exists as a dominant method, is the relationship between academia and practice. Praxis was where you went. What has changed slightly or has corrupted that model now is the idea of theory. The pedagogy of academia has now focused on theory, for example in all the Ph.D. programs that are in architecture schools. And that's something to think about. Is the school to be set up to feed people into the practice or is it set up to open the discipline, to explore the knowledge of the discipline?

JK: You're against that opening?

PE: Not necessarily. There's a tension in the world with people who see the school of architecture as a way of preparing people for practice. There is a difference, for example, if you go to a business school or for a Ph.D. in economics. There's an enormous difference between the Yale law school and the Harvard law school because they prepare people differently for practice. And these differences exist in architecture schools. I think Princeton is a school that's much more concerned about the discipline, whereas Harvard is much more concerned about the possibilities of practice. Yale is somewhere in between. I don't want to say that's good or bad. But I truly believe there has been a difference in pedagogy precisely because of the interest in theory that has developed in this country. And whether that's a good thing or bad thing remains to be seen.

Paradise Extension: True Confessions of a 21st-Century Objectivist

Mack Scogin

Options Studio, Spring 2008 **Students:** Jennifer Bonner, Carlos Cabrera, Michelle Chang, Sabeen Hasan, Justin Huxol, Edward Huyck, Patrick Jones, Jihoon Kim, Kevin Lee, Youngsu Lee, Jennifer Myers, Diane Rhyu, David Shanks. **Teaching Assistant:** Helen Han. **Participants:** Sarah Goldhagen, Dave Hickey, Jeffrey Kipnis.

The B-120 Wraith motorcycle is designed and manufactured by the Confederate Motor Company of Birmingham, Alabama. I find it to be an extraordinary object. For over six months now I have had on my desk a picture of it that was published in, of all things, *Surface* magazine. I decided to call the person who made it, Matt Chambers, to see what (or if) he was thinking when he designed it. He immediately started talking about Rembrandt, Jesse James (the one married to Sandra Bullock), automobile logos, Alexander Calder, the solar system, and Ayn Rand. He said he wasn't interested in things that were simply pretty. He firmly believes his motorcycle design is "ideologically driven" and that it "touches the soul."

I think it is very difficult to make anything today that touches the soul, transforms the pretty into the beautiful, is at once rigorously calculated and honest, and is inherently contradictory.

The aim of this studio was to investigate what each student participating believes to be their objects of desire: the values, function, form, language of visual effect, or other instruments of meaning they embody, and how these beliefs may inform a personal architecture. The fundamental exercise was to take a critical look at the cultural signifiers produced today, their meanings, their origins, and ultimately how we want them to evolve.

The studio collectively looked for more questions than answers while simultaneously seeking to define a personal position within the larger discourse, and eventually to design an architecture that addressed that position. Normative definitions of object, architecture, and meaning were expected to be challenged, if not transformed.

Antique Reptile, Priscus tersum

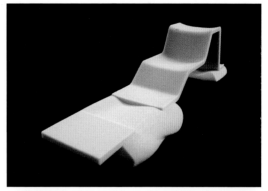

Floating Hydraulic Mattress, Habitat for Antique Reptile

Rain Maker, Pulvia formata

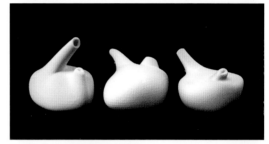

Filtration Buoys, Habitat for Rain Maker

Remora, Remora

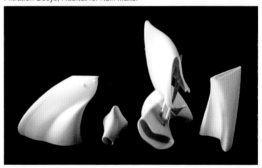

Clothes Line, Habitat for Remora

Levee Building, Tumulus condo

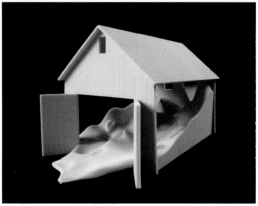

Muddy Barn, Habitat for Levee Builder

View standing on top of sheathed roof

Roof plates

Services network

Lattice structure

Shelter / Performance pods

Guard / Guidelines

Floor plates

Membrane soft space

Rigid stone

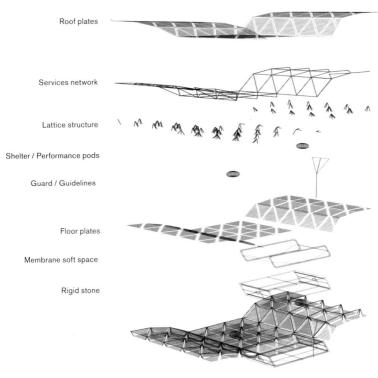

Tactics for inhabitation

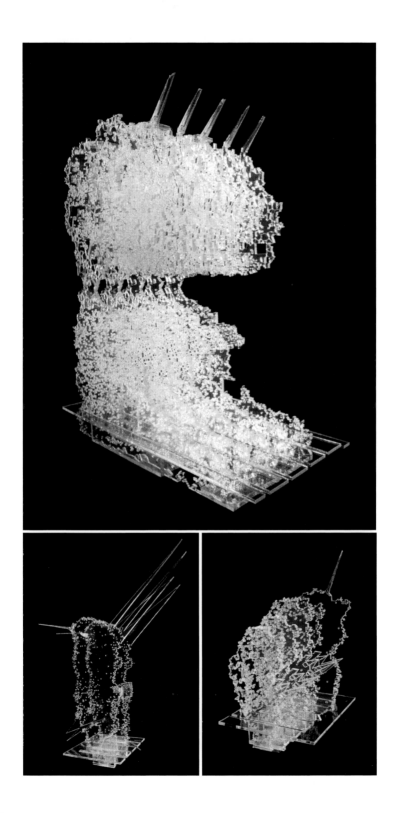

Excerpt: The Pipeline: Power, Infrastructure, Territory

Rania Ghosn
DDes Essay, 2008

Petroleum is the quintessential modern natural resource, a global commodity that is often removed and moved to distant places. Although technologies using fossil fuels have shaped the urban environment, the world economy, and the global landscape over the past two centuries, the connection between the transportation of energy and the production of the contemporary environment has been relatively underaddressed. At the intersection of political, economic, environmental, and technical considerations, pipelines have been discussed as objects of negotiation in foreign policy and between private oil firms and national economies, mostly overlooking the material relation between pipelines and the environment. Pipelines, however, embody a triad of nature, infrastructure, and power that allows us to examine the repercussions of the petroleum industry on geographies across spatial scales. Cross-border pipelines in particular have significantly impacted the physical and imaginary production of regional space: they have mapped and conquered frontier lands, brought about new cities or reconfigured the role of existing ones, while redrawing trade flows, property rights, pumping stations, ecological environments, regional transport services, highways and ports, and political relations across these territories.

As an infrastructure which brings a natural resource to the urban environment, the pipeline highlights the role of technology networks in the transformation of nature into the city and vice versa. Insuring the circulatory function of capital, large-scale engineering projects such as highways, railways, and pipelines "have to be immobilized in space, in order to facilitate greater movement for the remainder"[1]; they fix capital in the landscape, "shrink" distances, and organize the territory to increase the speed of resources, commodities, information, and people. Landscapes of technology thus materialize a will to dominate the earth, its resources and distances, and present telling stories of the interaction between technology, politics, and the environment.

Although academic literature has addressed the importance of the operational, economic, and social role of technology networks—water canals, railroads, streetcars, gas pipes, dams, electric cables, and pipelines—in the functioning of the modern city, their cultural, ideological, and aesthetic role has been largely overlooked. This is not surprising given their visual absence from contemporary cities.[2] Despite their importance for the functioning of the contemporary city, technology networks are today largely opaque or invisible: disappearing underground or locked into pipes, cables, conduits, tubes, passages, and electronic waves.

It has also been argued that the hidden form of contemporary technological infrastructures has contributed to severing the processes of the social transformation of nature from the processes of urbanization, further blurring the tense relationship between nature and the city.[3] This project adopts and builds upon an understanding

of urbanization as a "socioecological metabolism," whereby *social process*, *material metabolism*, and *spatial form* interweave to form landscapes. As such, socioecological processes produce both a new urban and rural socio-nature through complex networks of circulatory systems. This literature draws on the works of William Cronon, Neil Smith, and David Harvey, in tracing the role of technology, nature, and capital in the production of the urban from the exploitation of nature through the extraction of resources to the exchange of commodities through transport infrastructures. Cronon, for example, tells the story of Chicago from the vantage point of the socionatural processes and circulating flows that transform both city and countryside, demonstrating the extent of this process beyond the city's political border (and indeed beyond national borders).[4]

While histories of infrastructure have developed understandings of how infrastructural and societal change intertwine, they have done so mostly within national frameworks of analysis, almost completely neglecting transnational issues, or else focusing on their integrative aspect, as in the case of European examples. However, transport infrastructures have a significant colonial history as the tools of international private companies and foreign governments acting upon local interests, competing to monopolize access to energy and divide up Third World resources. Exceeding the capacity of a single state to provide for, in the postcolonial context transnational infrastructures raise issues of sovereignty between the state, global capital, international organizations, and local populations in a struggle over the routing, operation, and revenues of these lines. While annihilating boundaries for the frictionless flow of resources, these transnational infrastructures intersect political boundaries (for example, those of newly independent states in the post-World War II context), negotiate with states for power over their territories, and operate to draw states into, or away from, the orbit of powerful regional actors.

Furthermore, the spatial fixity of these infrastructures calls upon a political fixity among the countries they cross, deploying the tactics and strategies of power through "implantations, distributions, demarcations, control of territories, and organizations of domains."[5] As infrastructural networks immobilize capital and redraw flows in the landscape, they produce new territorial configurations and harness social processes in a new geography of places and relations. Particularly with respect to transport planning, scholars have increasingly recognized the importance of politics and the inseparability of planning from policy questions, technological history, and geopolitical concerns. The choice of routing for pipelines, for example, is an interesting example of this political process. As pipelines are extremely capital-intensive and present a high degree of inflexibility, the planning phase of pipeline routes is important, for once a pipeline is built, its route cannot be changed and its operation redefines the geography, development, and power balance of its region. Furthermore, the choice of pipeline routes does not necessarily chart the most economic route of transporting energy over land but raises the complex strategic, political, international, and social implications of projected routes.

To sustain the flow of capital, and in spite of repetitive episodes of war, the discourse on infrastructure relies on a political fix and a utopian imagination of peace and economic cooperation. In 1833, the Saint-Simonian and future French minister Michel Chevalier singled out railways as the ultimate tool to tie peoples and countries into interdependency, cooperation, and peace: "Railways have more relation to the religious spirit than we think... Never has there existed an instrument of such power to link together scattered peoples."[6] Chevalier's writings mark the full articulation of what has been called "the ideology of circulation," according to which "networks" discursively articulate mutual cooperation and understanding in the service of joint prosperity and peace. Transnational infrastructures thus require an imagined regional geography to legitimatize their existence, while simultaneously shaping the geography of the territory through their materiality and the promises they embody. While regions are significantly shaped by ideas or discourse, transnational spaces are not simply "imagined communities," but materialize and produce a desired geography of development and conflicts across local, national, and regional scales.

The globalization of oil as a commodity has embedded oil-producing regions and transnational infrastructures in geopolitical discourses and practices of energy security. Over the past decade, scarcity of resources, security threats on "critical infrastructure projects," and the discovery of hydrocarbon reserves in land-locked regions have brought the transport and security of energy into the foreground. While discourses on energy security have emphasized the military dimension of security practices, the oil crisis of the 1970s, the "oil wars" of the 1980s and 1990s, and post-September 11th discourses on the security of "critical infrastructures" have increasingly brought the discussion of security into non-military areas, such as the environment or the economy. Though generally portrayed as a technological-engineering problem, urbanizing nature is in fact as much part of the politics of life as any other social process. As cities are produced through socioecological processes, the political processes through which urban conditions are made and energy is transported question who produces what kind of socioecological configurations, and for whom.

1   David Harvey, "The Geopolitics of Capitalism," p. 149.
2   Maria Kaika, *City of Flows: Modernity, Nature, and the City* (New York, London: Routledge, 2005), p. 28.
3   Nik Heynen, Maria Kaika, and Erik Swyngedouw, eds., *In the Nature of Cities: Urban Political Ecology and the Politics of Urban Metabolism* (London, New York: Routledge, 2006).
4   William Cronon, *Nature's Metropolis: Chicago and the Great West* (New York: Norton, 1992); Neil Smith, *Uneven Development: Nature, Capital, and the Production of Space* (New York:

Blackwell, 1984); David Harvey, "The Geopolitics of Capitalism," in Derek Gregory and John Urry, eds., *Social Relations and Spatial Structures* (Basingstoke, Hampshire: Macmillan, 1985).
5   Michel Foucault, *Power/Knowledge: Selected Interviews and Other Writings 1972–1977* (Brighton, Sussex: Harvester Press, 1980), p. 77.
6   Van der Vleuten et al., "Europe's System Builders: The Contested Shaping of Transnational Road, Electricity and Rail Networks," *Contemporary European History*, vol.16.3 (2007), pp 321-347.

Excerpt: The Evolution of Designers as Global Actors in Fast-Growing Cities of the "Rest"

Shelagh McCartney
DDes Essay, 2008

The globalizing city has made new demands on the designer and, like other ages in history, requires new propositions to address the tensions of this new context. As contexts change, so does the role of designers. In the past, architects have responded after the fact to the social sciences in their building practices. In the current globalizing world, however, there is a need for designers to make propositions rather than reactions to the past, by examining the new form of the global context and using their imagination and skills to multitask. A documentation of the development of designers as global actors in the context of fast-growing, globalizing cities of "the Rest"—the so-called Third World—reveals the effects of globalization on rapidly growing cities, the phenomenon of informal self-built urbanization, and the need for designers in these contexts.

Globalization in its literal sense is the process by which localized phenomena are transformed into global phenomena. While the term is often used to refer to economic globalization, its definition should not be limited to economics alone. Thomas L. Friedman refers to the "flattening" of the globe, arguing that globalized trade and political forces have changed the world permanently, for better or worse. He argues that the pace of globalization is quickening and will continue to have a growing impact on business organizations and practices.[1] Noam Chomsky argues that the term "globalization" is used in a doctrinal sense to describe the neoliberal form of economic globalization.[2] Gordon Mathis, in his landmark analysis "Understanding the Postmodern World," postulates that globalization constitutes a revolution in the way people and societies transmit and analyze information. Herman E. Daly adds that while the terms "internationalization" and "globalization" are used interchangeably, there is a formal difference between them: internationalization refers to the importance of international trade, relations and treaties between or among nations, while globalization infers the erasure of national boundaries for economic purposes; international trade (governed by comparative advantages) becomes interregional trade (governed by absolute advantages).[3]

In current literature, much of the analysis and descriptions of this new globalized context has come by way of economics, human geography, and social anthropology. Kwame Anthony Appiah views citizenship participation through its relation to consumer capacity. Ulrich Beck examines the development of a globalized society as a "risk society" which creates occurrences during its development (for example, air pollution) that could alter all of humanity; once these occurrences have taken place, society relies on technology to fix the very problems that it initially created. Arjun Appadurai has also explored the definition of imagination and the field of possibility as a global actor, claiming that the world is currently being altered through five dimensions of global cultural flow: ethnoscapes, mediascapes, technoscapes, financescapes, and ideoscapes.

In the period since World War II a global shift has occurred as many countries have gained sovereignty from their colonizers and large-scale rural-to-urban migration has taken place. Migration has caused widespread and unplanned urbanization as a massive succession of individual incidents that have gradually transformed a seemingly incontrovertible order. Populations migrate from rural agricultural areas to the city for reasons that include property rights issues in the countryside, security from civil war, agricultural crises, lower infant mortality, better wages, the growth of government bureaucracy, or the potential of obtaining a better education. Cities have become heavily populated metropolises with new and unfamiliar neighborhoods. New activities have emerged and replaced traditional ones. A new paradigm of city-making is occurring.

Today, cities have reached sizes that are historically unprecedented. While there are examples in the history of cities of populations of 1 million or more inhabitants, the city of several million inhabitants is a relatively new phenomenon. At the beginning of the 1900s, only sixteen cities worldwide had populations larger than 1 million people. Yet at the beginning of the 2000s more than 500 cities had more than 1 million inhabitants– many boasting more than 10 million and still expanding. In 1800, the average size of the world's largest hundred cities was around 200,000, compared to 700,000 in 1900, 2.1 million in 1950, and roughly 5.1 million inhabitants in 1990.[4] In 2008, the world reached an invisible but momentous milestone: for the first time in history, more than half of its human population (equal to 3.3 billion people) will live in urban areas, a figure the United Nations Population Fund (UNFPA) expects to swell to 5 billion by the year 2030.

Historically, Asia has always had a high proportion of the world's largest cities. In 2005, twenty-eight of the world's fifty cities with over 5 million inhabitants were in Asia, and this proportion is likely to increase, reflecting its increasing weight within the world economy. North America and sub-Saharan Africa stand out as having the most "new" large cities—settlements that had not been founded or did not exist as urban centers before 1800. In 1900, Europe had more than half of the world's hundred largest cities; today it only has twenty-seven of the world's 500 cities with a population over 1 million, whereas 179 of them are in countries of the Rest. It is predicted that by 2015, eighteen cities will have 10 million inhabitants, all but three of them in the Rest. A fundamental difference from the growth trends of past cities is that these were based primarily upon industrialization within their own country, rather than through the forces of globalization that are currently causing growth in the cities of the Rest. The most pervasive element in rapidly developing cities is the phenomenon of informal urbanization, which has achieved a demographic and territorial importance that cannot be ignored. Populations have built and upgraded on the edges of urban areas for centuries, and these communities have matured to become valuable parts of the city. What has changed in recent times is the scale of these areas due to continuing urban migration. With one of every two urban dwellers predicted to be living in slum conditions by 2025, more than one and a half billion people may be expected to live in areas of informal urbanization.

Despite an increased interest in informal settlements, it is surprising that so little research has been conducted outside of the realm of housing policy, especially from a perspective beyond the needs of individual citizens. Existing research on the physical needs of the city has been especially scarce. Very few studies have focused on how planners and communities in informal settlements can contribute to the integration of the city as a whole, and on related implications for preserving scarce resources and minimizing the adverse impacts of development, the realm in which physical planners can contribute the most.[5] In the recent history of developing countries, there is an important but underestimated link between design and planning and their interaction with development procedures.

This interaction transforms the idea of what defines a city and challenges the notions of urban planning and redevelopment best practices. The urban fringe is no longer an insignificant site occupied by a minority but a strategic space in and around cities, occupied by an informal majority, where the future development of the city will take place. While creative and informal solutions have thus far provided the primary solutions for housing at the level of the individual resident, the modalities of informal settlements have wasted land and services which represent a cost to all of society. The physical design of our homes, neighborhoods, and communities shapes every aspect of our lives. Yet architects are too often desperately needed in the places where they can least be afforded or are the least available.

Many of the world's rapidly growing cities are located in territories that gained sovereignty or underwent a significant shift in political systems after World War II. These cities were previously dominated by colonial rule where experts of the ruling imperial power controlled the systems and implementation of formal building and city design. In the rapid development of cities today, international systems and standards are needed to ensure general safety in dense multistory developments. The current number of designers in these cities is very low, and there is clearly a need for more architects in order to keep pace with the demand for rapid growth.[6]

Recent literature indicates that in many of these rapidly growing centers the most iconic buildings are given to international architects for their design and technical expertise. High-profile jobs have found themselves at the drawing boards (or rather, computer screens) of foreign offices, while many local young architects who leave their countries to receive education and experience do not return. While in every rapidly growing city there are iconic buildings, it is often overlooked that the remainder of the city fabric, including housing, yields a much greater construction investment.

Traditionally designers have worked primarily as agents, with the authority to act in the place of the parties that hire them. Prior to the major shift towards a globalizing economy, designers typically acted as individuals or as part of firms of fewer than twenty people. Shifts in technology, economic flows, and the emergence of other actors have enabled designers today to become global actors themselves. Understanding this evolution provides the means to decipher and leverage how designers can transform their role and prepare future generations who will practice in this area and define the future as facilitators.

Growth pattern in Istanbul, c. 2008

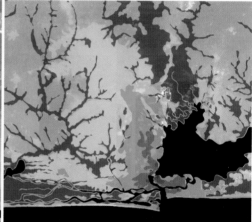

Growth pattern in Lagos, c. 2008

1   Thomas L. Friedman, *The World Is Flat: A Brief History of the Twenty-First Century* (New York: Farrar, Straus and Giroux, 2007).
2   "Corporate Globalization, Korea and International Affairs: Noam Chomsky interviewed by Sun Woo Lee," *Monthly Joong Ang* (ZNet), February 22, 2006.
3   Herman E. Daly, "Globalization versus Internationalization—Some Implications," *Ecological Economics* 31 (1999), pp. 31–37.
4   Tertius Chandler, *Four Thousand Years of Urban Growth: An Historical Census* (Cardiff: St. David's University Press, 1987).
5   See Mona Serageldin, *Regularizing the Informal Land Development Process* (Washington, D.C.: USAID, 1990), and Jose Manuel Castillo, *Urbanisms of the Informal: Spatial Transformations in the Urban Fringe of Mexico City* (Cambridge, 2000).

6   At the extreme low end are Rwanda, where there are six architects working in a population of 10 million (0.599 architects per million); Nigeria, with 2,360 architects working for 151 million people (15.58 per million); and Malaysia, with approximately 1,600 architects—the same number as a decade ago—working for 27 million people (59.20 architects per million). Compare this to the United States. In 1850, when the U.S. population was primarily rural, there were thirty architects per million people. In the early 1900s, when U.S. cities began to increase rapidly in size due to industrialization, there were approximately 175 architects per million people. After World War II in a globalizing economy, there were over 600 architects per million people.

Excerpt: NOW?

Arjun Appadurai
Dialogue, April 8, 2008

I have often been criticized as being a victim of a sort of breathless "now"-ism, itself seen as a product of historical illiteracy, Pollyannaish optimism, and a naïve belief in the powers of the imagination. This critique, which takes many forms, usually comes from self-appointed custodians of the "then," usually told as some sort of fable of the steady degeneration of industrial capitalism. On examination, these same critics also turn out to have a fixed menu of offerings for "what comes next," which is usually a derivative of the same fable. So I am happy to say a few things about the politics of now as I see it in my current situation and interest.

We are engaged now in a very serious effort to start, with no prior prejudices, a dialogue between design and the social sciences—both words conceived very broadly—with a focus, firstly, on what were referred to in the early 1980s as "wicked problems" in urban planning; secondly, on issues pertaining to sustainability and adaptation, rather than simply mitigation; thirdly, on the independent design of contexts. I will repeat: on the independent design of contexts as such, rather than just of objects, large or small, in the hope that salutary or sustainable contexts will simply follow.

This project, which is very young and very new, forces all of us in this dialogue between the social sciences and design to rethink our ideas of form, style, and scale, as well as of markets, consumers, and not least, pedagogies. This project has helped me to build on my earlier interest in what I refer to as the social life of things, building on those things to move towards a direct dialogue with design and planning. I hope and know many of you will probably shape that dialogue in the decade or more to come.

My second recent interest comes out of an older interest also in the dialogue between anthropology and economics, especially as regards economic development and what some have called ethical globalization. Here my recent work on housing activists and their work, particularly in Mumbai and secondarily in South Africa, the Philippines, and in numerous other countries, has drawn me deep into the question of what I have called deep democracy in one essay; of the capacity to aspire, the title of another essay coming out; and of what, in a third essay, I call cosmopolitanism from below.

All these are premised on the idea that all human beings are designers by necessity, and that professional design—Design—is always an intervention in what, in my book *Modernity at Large*, I call the production of locality by design as an engine of ordinary life. In that book I talked about the production of locality, but now we could say that

locality—or what others would call the everyday, or ordinary life—is produced by the activity of design as its central engine. Design not only disturbs the flow of things; it is not a process enacted on a tabula rasa. It is even more important to say that Design intervenes already in design, as the engine of the production of the ordinary. By this I mean something more than simply non-intentional design. I mean to say that ordinary people reproduce everyday life at very high cost by acts of design all the time. If Design doesn't understand that it's already intervening in design, already it becomes very difficult.

This body of work that I have tried to produce based on my contacts with housing activists, and therefore with slum planners and ordinary very poor people—the poorest of the urban poor in Mumbai and many other similar cities—has roots in my earlier interest in the imagination as a social practice, a phrase that I use in *Modernity at Large*, and has gradually morphed into a much deeper and broader collective project on what I call the anthropology of the future.

This project is premised on the idea that anthropology—used broadly to mean anybody who takes this kind of ethnographically grounded, culturally-oriented approach—has remained deeply anchored (profitably, even) in issues of memory, history, tradition, habit, habitus, and other such terms of reference to the past, and has largely handed the future over to other fields. I mean primarily economics and related fields, and only secondarily planning, design, and so on. This has led to great results, and while there are people who welcome the present in anthropology, on the whole, this is a very small slice of the anthropological pie. I believe it is now time to recognize that anthropology has much to add to the subjects of imagination, anticipation, prediction, projection, risk, and uncertainty. This comes back to the dialogue between anthropology and design, because it positions anthropology not as the "other" of fields that want to intervene in the future, but as a partner if we bring something to the table.

If you look at the archive of anthropology going back a century, there are great thinkers and great work. It's not that the future is not present; you can point it out in many, many fields. But it has so far, as a field, failed to take systematic account of what Clifford Geertz might have called—but unfortunately didn't—the future as a cultural fact. We think of religion as a cultural fact, or ideology as a cultural fact; but the future as a cultural fact is spread out in the literature, but has not been pulled together for the purpose of further work.

My own interests in this project have led me to make a distinction cut into the anthropology of the future, which is of special interest to me now but is not, by any means, something that defines or exhausts the field. It is a distinction between two ethics: what are called, contrastively, the ethics of probability and the ethics of possibility.

The ethics of probability is part of the technologies of state, market, and the mindless exploitation of nature. It is an ethic that has its roots in what Ian Hacking called the "avalanche of numbers"; what James Scott saw, in a different way, as the basic feature of "seeing like a state" in his famous phrase; and which Foucault saw as the capillary consequence of the panoptical tools of census, diagnostic or disease nosologies, and other techniques for manipulating biopower in the interests of governmentality. This is the ethics that today dominates the large hedge funds, those who play in nature's casino with instruments like catastrophe bonds (which, if you haven't heard of, I suggest you find out about), and those who, as Naomi Klein has recently shown in her book *The Shock Doctrine*, use catastrophe as a planned tool for future profit. Against this ethic, the ethics of possibility emphasizes the capacities of ordinary citizens for making their own designs for the future, building their own resources for strengthening the sinews of hope—what I call the capacity to aspire, which I think is a buildable capacity like any other capacity that we seek to build—and their own networked ability to organize their powers for more ethical forms of globalization, which stress locality, sustainability, and inclusion.

Let us join in opening a space for the ethics of possibility. Otherwise, we will simply drown, contingently, in the workings of the ethics of probability.

Design, with its relatively short-term views, needs some of the lofty future orientation that planners tend to bring to all projects. But—lest you think that planning for me is the top of the pile that now regulates the whole world—planning itself, I believe, needs to become more humble, more local, more vernacular, and more democratic. Planners need to learn a bit about style, consumption, display, and embodied pleasure. This is no easy task, but if this triangular relationship between fashion, design, and planning can be worked out thoughtfully, critically, collectively, and collaboratively, then design might resume its rightful pride of place as the agora where social science, engineering, and art, broadly conceived, can make their most lasting contribution to a world worth sustaining.

These comments are about how we can move forward to work for the betterment of things, from the point of view of cities, poverty, equity, and development, without trivializing design with a lower-case D, and somehow seeing planning as a lofty thing, but to create a different dialogue. Here, social science and ideas like the anthropology of the future can help.

How do we do that together? It is a reminder that one has to also keep a very critical eye on the forces that are producing the ethics of probability. It is not enough to move in a more positive direction; one has to keep doing the work of critique, about things we think we know but are always worth returning to and reexamining more deeply.

Drew Gilpin Faust
President of Harvard University

HARVARD GRADUATE SCHOOL OF DESIGN

Mohsen Mostafavi
Dean of the Faculty of Design

Alan A. Altshuler
Dean of the Faculty of Design, 2005–2007

Patricia J. Roberts
Executive Dean

Preston Scott Cohen
Chair, Department of Architecture;
Director, Master in Architecture Degree Programs, 2006–2007

Toshiko Mori
Chair, Department of Architecture, 2002–2008

Niall G. Kirkwood
Chair, Department of Landscape Architecture;
Director, Master in Landscape Architecture Degree Programs, 2005–2008

Rodolfo Machado
Co-Chair, Department of Urban Planning and Design

Jerold S. Kayden
Co-Chair, Department of Urban Planning and Design;
Director, Master in Urban Planning Degree Program

Monica Ponce de Leon
Director, Master in Architecture Degree Programs, Spring 2008

Christian Werthmann
Director, Master in Landscape Architecture Degree Programs

Richard M. Sommer
Director, Master of Architecture in Urban Design Degree Program;
Director, Master of Landscape Architecture in Urban Design Program

Daniel L. Schodek
Director, Master in Design Studies Degree Program

FACULTY OF DESIGN

Alan A. Altshuler, Ruth and Frank Stanton Professor in Urban Policy and Planning
George Baird, G. Ware Travelstead Professor of Architecture Emeritus
John Beardsley, Senior Lecturer in Landscape Architecture
Martin Bechthold, Professor of Architecture
Alan Berger, Associate Professor of Landscape Architecture
Eve Blau, Adjunct Professor of Architectural History
Michael Blier, Design Critic in Landscape Architecture
Joan Busquets, Martin Bucksbaum Professor in Practice of Urban Planning and Design
Marco Cenzatti, Lecturer in Urban Planning
Holly Getch Clarke, Associate Professor of Landscape Architecture
Preston Scott Cohen, Gerald M. McCue Professor of Architecture
Leland D. Cott, Adjunct Professor of Urban Design
Margaret Crawford, Professor of Urban Design and Planning Theory
Peter Del Tredici, Lecturer in Landscape Architecture
Richard A. Dimino, Lecturer in Urban Planning and Design

Frederick Edward Smith, Professor of Advanced Environmental Studies in Resources and Ecology Emeritus
Laura Solano, Lecturer in Landscape Architecture
Richard M. Sommer, Associate Professor of Architecture and Urban Design
Marco Steinberg, Associate Professor of Architecture
Carl F. Steinitz, Alexander and Victoria Wiley Research Professor of Landscape Architecture and Planning
John R. Stilgoe, Robert and Lois Orchard Professor in the History of Landscape Development
Kostas Terzidis, Associate Professor of Architecture
Maryann Thompson, Adjunct Professor of Architecture
Matthew Urbanski, Lecturer in Landscape Architecture
Michael R. Van Valkenburgh, Charles Eliot Professor in Practice of Landscape Architecture
François C. D. Vigier, Charles Dyer Norton Professor of Regional Planning Emeritus
Charles Ward Harris, Professor of Landscape Architecture Emeritus
Christian Werthmann, Associate Professor of Landscape Architecture
Jay Wickersham, Lecturer in Architecture
T. Kelly Wilson, Adjunct Associate Professor of Architecture
Martin Zogran, Assistant Professor of Urban Design

VISITING FACULTY

Kimberly Ackert, Design Critic in Architecture
Daniel Adams, Design Critic in Urban Planning and Design
Eric Belsky, Lecturer in Urban Planning and Design
Brian Blaesser, Lecturer in Urban Planning and Design
Sibel Bozdogan, Lecturer in Architecture
Angelo Bucci, Design Critic in Architecture
Thomas Campanella, Visiting Assistant Professor of Urban Planning and Design
Charles Canon, Design Critic in Landscape Architecture
Armando Carbonell, Design Critic in Urban Planning and Design
Steven Cecil, Design Critic in Urban Planning and Design
Jane Choi, Design Critic in Landscape Architecture
Nazneen Cooper, Design Critic in Landscape Architecture
Marcela Correa, Design Critic in Architecture
Felipe Correa, Design Critic in Urban Planning and Design
Paul Cote, Lecturer in Landscape Architecture, Urban Planning and Design
Lise Anne Couture, Kenzo Tange Design Critic in Architecture
Teddy Cruz, Design Critic in Architecture
Winka Dubbeldam, Design Critic in Architecture
Ana Maria Duran, Design Critic in Architecture
Stephen Ervin, Lecturer in Landscape Architecture
Kristin Frederickson, Design Critic in Landscape Architecture
Scheri Fultineer, Design Critic in Landscape Architecture
Shauna Gillies-Smith, Design Critic in Landscape Architecture
Laura Gornowski, Teaching Associate in Landscape Architecture
Toni Griffin, Design Critic in Urban Planning and Design
Eric Howeler, Design Critic in Architecture
Louisa Hutton, Design Critic in Architecture
Florian Idenburg, Design Critic in Architecture
Dominique Jakob, Design Critic in Architecture
Flavio Janches, Design Critic in Landscape Architecture
Alice Jarrard, Lecturer in Architecture
Virginia Johnson, Design Critic in Landscape Architecture
Mark Kalin, Lecturer in Architecture
Hanif Kara, Design Critic in Architecture
Emma Kelly, Design Critic in Landscape Architecture
Sheila Kennedy, Design Critic in Architecture
Brian Kenet, Lecturer in Landscape Architecture
Matthew Kiefer, Lecturer in Urban Planning and Design
Jeffrey Kipnis, Visiting Professor of Architecture
Jeannette Kuo, Design Critic in Architecture
Sanford Kwinter, Visiting Associate Professor of Architecture
Inès Lamunière, Design Critic in Architecture

Sylvia Lavin, Visiting Professor of Architecture
Michael Lee, Lecturer in Landscape Architecture
Mia Lehrer, Design Critic in Landscape Architecture
Brendan MacFarlane, Design Critic in Architecture
Kathryn Madden, Design Critic in Urban Planning and Design
Francisco Mangado, Design Critic in Architecture
Robert Marino, Design Critic in Architecture
Katherine Martin, Design Critic in Landscape Architecture
Wilson Martin, Lecturer in Landscape Architecture
Ryue Nishizawa, Kenzo Tange Visiting Professor in Architecture
Nicholas Pouder, Design Critic in Landscape Architecture
Smiljan Radic, Design Critic in Architecture
Hani Rashid, Kenzo Tange Design Critic in Architecture
Christoph Reinhart, Visiting Lecturer in Architecture
Nicolas Retsinas, Lecturer in Urban Planning and Design
Cheri Ruane, Design Critic in Landscape Architecture
Matthias Sauerbruch, Design Critic in Architecture
Michael Schroeder, Lecturer in Architecture
James Stockard, Lecturer in Urban Planning and Design
Renz van Luxemburg, Lecturer in Architecture
Juan Carlos Vargas-Moreno, Lecturer in Landscape Architecture
Craig Verzone, Design Critic in Landscape Architecture
Bing Wang, Lecturer in Urban Planning and Design
Jay Wickersham, Lecturer in Architecture
Sylvia Winter, Design Critic in Landscape Architecture

STAFF 2007–2008

Patricia Alves, Executive Education Administration
Robert Angilly, Library
Alla Armstrong, Academic Finance
Lauren Baccus, Director of Human Resources
Pamela Baldwin, Joint Center for Housing Studies
Kermit Baker, Joint Center for Housing Studies
Lauren Beath, Finance
Todd Belton, Computer Resources
Eric Belsky, Joint Center for Housing Studies
Amal Bendimerad, Joint Center for Housing Studies
Susan Boland-Kourdov, Computer Resources
Daniel Borelli, Exhibitions and Publications
Tamala Bothwell, Human Resources
Stacy Buckley, Executive Education Administration
Leslie Burke, Dean's Office
Kevin Cahill, Facilities Manager
Bonnie Campbell, Development
Anna Cimini, Computer Resources
Douglas Cogger, Computer Resources
Ellen Colleran, Urban Planning and Design
Sean Conlon, Registrar
Paul Cote, Computer Resources
Anne Creamer, Career Services
Andrea Croteau, Architecture
Maria Da Rosa, Library
Mary Daniels, Library
Aparna Das, Academic Affairs
Heather deManbey, Registrar
Zhu Xiao Di, Joint Center for Housing Studies
Sarah Dickinson, Library
Rachel Drew, Joint Center for Housing Studies
Kathryn Eaton, Faculty Planning
Barbara Elfman, Advanced Studies Programs

Mary England, Joint Center for Housing Studies
Stephen Ervin, Assistant Dean for Information Technology; Director, Computer Resources
Cynthia Fallows, Loeb Fellowship
Angela Flynn, Joint Center for Housing Studies
Adriana Forte, Landscape Architecture
Mary Fossey, Development
Heather Gallagher, Executive Education Administration
Keith Gnoza, Director of Financial Assistance
Meryl Golden, Director of Career Services
Desiree Goodwin, Library
Irina Gorstein, Library
Elizabeth Gould, Computer Resources
Harold Gould, Computer Resources
Norton Greenfeld, Development
Arin Gregorian, Academic Finance
Deborah Grohe, Building Services
Gail Gustafson, Director of Admissions
Mark Hagen, Computer Resources
Barry Harper, Building Services
Jill Harrington, Admissions
Deborah Harris, Communications
Amanda Heighes, Internal Publications
Jackie Hernandez, Joint Center for Housing Studies
Ariel Herwitz, Architecture
Stephen Hickey, Shop Facilities
Megan Homan, Development
Dennis Howe, Building Services
Nancy Jennings, Joint Center for Housing Studies
Deborah Johansen, Director of Communications
Johanna Kasubowski, Library
Adam Kellie, Library
Bohyun Kim, Library
Brooke Lynn King, Academic Affairs
Linda Kitch, Library
Karen Kittredge, Finance
Jeffrey Klug, Career Discovery
Grace Kulegian, Landscape Architecture
Kevin Lau, Library
Perrin LeBlanc, Executive Education Administration
Gina Lee, Architecture
Sharon Lembo, Real Estate Academic Initiative
Mary MacLean, Finance
Elaine Mar, Architecture
Daniel McCue, Joint Center for Housing Studies
Wesley McGee, Shop Facilities
Michael McGrath, Director of Faculty Planning
Margaret Meaney, Architecture
Jessica Merenda, Real Estate Academic Initiative
Karin Min, Development
Barbara Mitchell, Library
Margaret Moore De Chicojay, Executive Education Administration
Corlette Moore McCoy, Director of Executive Education
Maria Moran, Academic Affairs
Gerilyn Nederhoff, Director of Admissions
Howard Nelson, Library
Zachary Newton, Urban Planning and Design
Margaret Nipson, Joint Center for Housing Studies
Bradley Niskanen, Computer Resources
Trevor O'Brien, Building Services
Clarissa Ocampo, Computer Resources
Maria Pantazis, Computer Resources
Kevin Park, Joint Center for Housing Studies

Hannah Peters, Associate Dean for External Relations External Relations
Jacqueline Piracini, Director of Administration for Academic Services
Pilar Raynor Jordan, Academic Finance
Julia Reiskind, Library
Nicolas Retsinas, Joint Center for Housing Studies
Michael Rejto, Computer Resources
Ann Renauer, Assistant Dean for Finance
Carlos Reyes, Academic Affairs
Patricia J. Roberts, Executive Dean, Academic Affairs
Rebecca Rose, Real Estate Academic Initiative
Janet Rutan, Library
Meghan Ryan, Harvard Design Magazine
William Saunders, Assistant Dean; Editor, Harvard Design Magazine
Paul Scannell, Building Services
Elizabeth Schwartz, Computer Resources
Emily Scudder, Library
Timothy Smith, Urban Planning and Design
Laura Snowdon, Assistant Dean for Student Services
Shannon Stecher, Exhibitions and Publications
James Stockard, Curator, Loeb Fellowship Program
Olga Strakhov, Library
Aimee Taberner, Landscape Architecture
Anna Taylor, Computer Resources
Kelly Teixeira, Student Services
Mark Torrey, Computer Resources
Kathan Tracy, Development
Laurel Trayes, Joint Center for Housing Studies
Jennifer Vallone, Finance
Edna Van Saun, Assistant Director of Alumni Relations
Melissa Vaughn, Director of Exhibitions and Publications
Jessica Walton, Real Estate Academic Initiative
Juliet Wendel, Student Services
Hugh Wilburn, Assistant Dean for Information Services; Librarian
Sara Wilkinson, Human Resources
Abbe Will, Joint Center for Housing Studies
Janet Wysocki, Executive Education Administration
Sarah Young, Loeb Fellowship
Ines Zalduendo, Library
Natalie Zalkin, External Relations
Mendel Zou, Library

IMAGE CREDITS

Anita Kan: Inside front cover, 45, 78–79, 81 (top), 98 (bottom), 125, 128–129, 136, 142 (top), 189, 194–195, 202, 208, 219, 239, inside back cover
Doug Cogger: 8–9, 68–72, 190–193
Ivan Shumkov: 20 (top)
Andrei Gheorghe: 20 (bottom), 103
Google Maps: 25
Ron Witte: 30
Yusun Kwon: 41, 81 (bottom), 87, 90
Ronan Bouroullec: 49 (Algae: right; Clips, left)
Ronan and Erwan Bouroullec: 48 (Algae: left; Rock: left, middle, right; Tiles: left, middle, right), 49 (Rock: left, middle, right; Tiles: right)
Paul Tahon: 48 (Algae: middle; Clips: left, middle, right), 49 (Algae: left, middle)

Paul Tahon and Ronan and Erwan Bouroullec: 48 (Algae: right), 49 (Clips: middle, right; Tiles, left, middle)
Sylvia Feng: 105
Kostas Terzidis: 157
Ingeborg Rocker: 159–161
David Gale: 163 (top)
Bryan Boyer: 165–167, 170–171, 174 (bottom), 218
Christian Werthmann: 187
Sheila Kennedy: 197
Edward Lifson: 221
Rania Ghosn: 231
Shelagh McCartney: 237

Mohsen Mostafavi
Dean, Faculty of Design

Alan A. Altshuler
Dean, Faculty of Design, 2005–2007

Preston Scott Cohen
Chair, Department of Architecture

Toshiko Mori
Chair, Department of Architecture, 2002–2008

Niall Kirkwood
Chair, Department of Landscape Architecture

Rodolfo Machado
Co-Chair, Department of Urban Planning and Design

Jerold Kayden
Co-Chair, Department of Urban Planning and Design

FACULTY EDITOR FOR GSD 08 PLATFORM
Lluís Ortega
Assistant Professor of Architecture

CONSULTING EDITOR
Michael Kubo

STUDENT EDITORS
Noel Murphy
Bryan Boyer
Joshua Dannenberg

GSD 08 Platform represents selected studios, seminars, research, events, and exhibitions from the 2007–2008 academic year.

For additional information and a more comprehensive selection of student work, see www.gsd.harvard.edu/studioworks.

The Harvard Graduate School of Design is a leading center for education, information, and technical expertise on the built environment. Its Departments of Architecture, Landscape Architecture, and Urban Planning and Design offer masters and doctoral degree programs and provide the foundation for the School's Advanced Studies and Executive Education.

ISBN 978-1-934510-16-2

Library of Congress Cataloging-in-Publication Data

Ortega, Lluís.
  GSD 08 platform / Lluís Ortega.
  250 p., 15,2 x 22,9 cm.
  Includes bibliographical references.
  ISBN 978-1-934510-16-2 (alk. paper)
  1. Architecture–Research–Massachusetts–Cambridge. 2. Architectural Design–Research–Massachusetts–Cambridge. 3. Harvard University. Graduate School of Design. I. Title.

NA2300.H352O78 2008
724'.7–dc22
2008036604

PUBLISHED BY
Harvard University Graduate School of Design
Actar

ACKNOWLEDGMENTS

This publication would not have been possible without the efforts of the following people:

Mohsen Mostafavi
Pat Roberts
Melissa Vaughn
Dan Borelli
Stephen Ervin
Toshiko Mori
Christian Werthmann
Richard Sommer
Daniel Schodek
Antoine Picon
Hashim Sarkis
Sean Conlon
Kate Eaton
Mike McGrath

DESIGN
Ramon Prat (Actar)
Reinhard Steger (Actar)
Celia Costa (Actar)

COPY EDITOR
Amanda Heighes

ART COLLECTION AND PREPARATION MANAGER
Shannon Stecher

ART COLLECTION AND PREPARATION
Matthew Allen
Frank Braman
David Stuart Zimmerman

TECHNICAL CONSULTING
Todd Belton

MODEL, EXHIBITION, AND EVENT PHOTOGRAPHY
Anita Kan (unless otherwise noted)

DISTRIBUTION
Actar D
Roca i Batlle 2–4
08023 Barcelona
T +34 93 4171993
F +34 934186707
office@actar-d.com
www.actar-d.com

DISTRIBUTION USA
Actar Distribution Inc
158 Lafayette St. 5th Floor
New York, NY 10013
T +1 212 9662207
F +1 212 9662214
officeusa@actar-d.com
www.actar-d.com